S0-ABD-300

Here is a wise, gentle, Bible-based, low-key introduction and discussion-starter on a matter of huge importance for Christian credibility in this generation. May it be widely read, and taken deeply to heart.

—J. I. Packer, D. Phil., Board of Governors
and Professor, Regent College, Vancouver

A PUBLIC FAITH

Bringing Personal Faith to Public Issues

CHARLES DREW

NAVPRESS
BRINGING TRUTH TO LIFE
P.O. Box 35001, Colorado Springs, Colorado 80935

OUR GUARANTEE TO YOU

We believe so strongly in the message of our books that we are making this quality guarantee to you. If for any reason you are disappointed with the content of this book, return the title page to us with your name and address and we will refund to you the list price of the book. To help us serve you better, please briefly describe why you were disappointed. Mail your refund request to: NavPress, P.O. Box 35002, Colorado Springs, CO 80935.

The Navigators is an international Christian organization. Our mission is to reach, disciple, and equip people to know Christ and to make Him known through successive generations. We envision multitudes of diverse people in the United States and every other nation who have a passionate love for Christ, live a lifestyle of sharing Christ's love, and multiply spiritual laborers among those without Christ.

NavPress is the publishing ministry of The Navigators. NavPress publications help believers learn biblical truth and apply what they learn to their lives and ministries. Our mission is to stimulate spiritual formation among our readers.

© 2000 by Charles D. Drew
All rights reserved. No part of this publication may be reproduced in any form without written permission from NavPress, P.O. Box 35001, Colorado Springs, CO 80935.
www.navpress.com
Library of Congress Catalog Card Number: 00-031877
ISBN 1-57683-215-5

Cover design by Stephen Eames
Cover photo from Photodisc, manipulation by Stephen Eames
Creative Team: Eric Stanford, Marla Kennedy, TSI Graphics

Some of the anecdotal illustrations in this book are true to life and are included with the permission of the persons involved. All other illustrations are composites of real situations, and any resemblance to people living or dead is coincidental.

Unless otherwise identified, all Scripture quotations in this publication are taken from the HOLY BIBLE: NEW INTERNATIONAL VERSION® (NIV®). Copyright © 1973, 1978, 1984 by International Bible Society. Used by permission of Zondervan Publishing House. All rights reserved. Other versions used include: The New English Bible (NEB), © 1961, 1970, The Delegates of the Oxford University Press and The Syndics of the Cambridge University Press;

Library of Congress Cataloging-in-Publication Data

Drew, Charles D., 1950-
    A public faith : a balanced approach to social and political action / Charles D. Drew.
      p. cm.
    Includes bibliographical references.
    ISBN 1-57683-215-5 (pbk.)
      1. Christianity and politics. 2. United States—Religion. I. Title.

BR115.P7 D74 2000
261.7'9073—dc21

00-031877

Printed in the United States of America

1 2 3 4 5 6 7 8 9 10 / 05 04 03 02 01 00

FOR A FREE CATALOG OF
NAVPRESS BOOKS & BIBLE STUDIES,
CALL 1-800-366-7788 (USA)
OR 1-416-499-4615 (CANADA)

CONTENTS

INTRODUCTION

"You're a Christian. You care about people. Throw a brick!" A fellow student fresh from battle with the police offered me a broken piece of mortar as he spoke. It was a spring evening in 1970, at the height of the Vietnam war, my sophomore year at Harvard. Tear gas hung in the muggy sky, stinging my eyes. Confused about the issue and unhappy with the proposed method of protest, I declined my friend's challenge and he moved on. But I did not forget what he said. As wrongheaded as he may have been regarding tactics, he was right in his assumption that because I was a Christian I had social obligations.

Twenty-two years later, as things began to heat up for the 1992 elections, I felt pressure from some of the members of my church to say something about our political involvement. Many of them had in mind that I'd give tacit endorsement to a particular party by exposing my people to voting records of various incumbents made available by the Christian Coalition. Others in my church were terrified that I might do just that, and urged me to keep out of politics. What was I, as a minister, to do? I knew that the people of my church should be involved. But was the power politics of the Christian Coalition the only, or preferred, way?

Not many months later a member of the local clergy association to which I belonged circulated for the association's discussion, modification, and eventual endorsement a paper on homosexuals in the military. The statement, which I did not sign, later appeared in the local newspaper. One of my parishioners, infuriated upon reading it, came to me, saying, "You know those guys, don't you?

Shouldn't you talk to them about this or issue some sort of refutation?" My friend seemed to make at least two assumptions — first, that I shared his sense of priority about the issue, and second, that the practical meaning of the biblical injunction against homosexual behavior was quite plain when applied to the question of gays in the military. How was I to explain that I did not share his assumptions without sounding somehow un-Christian?

How should Christians respond to what some have called the culture wars? Do we remove ourselves and wait for the Lord Jesus to come fix things? Or do we fight? And if we fight, where do we enlist, and against whom do we fight? Are the Democrats the bad guys, or are the Republicans? Is there a group to be found that is readily identifiable with the aims and standards of our heavenly King? And what do we do when we discover fellow Christians in the "wrong" army? How should we fight, and what sorts of weapons should we use?

These questions are not easily answered. Those who answer them too glibly polarize the church and lead it away from its principal tasks. Those who refuse to try to answer them avoid their responsibility to be salt and light in the world.

As I write in the summer of 1999, I cannot help but wonder if the respite Americans presently enjoy from internal strife is superficial, due largely to the remarkable economic prosperity we have been enjoying. The social history of the century we leave behind, full of unprecedented experiment and brutality, only confirms the Bible's teaching that human society is forever a volcano waiting to erupt. Serious-minded Christians cannot afford to withdraw from public life. It is not enough to enjoy vibrant worship, strong devotions, good relationships at work, and a happy family life — the sorts of things that most popular writing on the Christian life deals with.

But how can we be as serious about our public life as we are about our private life without tearing the church apart? How, in other words, can serious-minded Republicans, Democrats, and independents worship together under the same roof? This is the practical question that led me as a pastor to preach the series of sermons that later became this book. I write for Christians committed to the authority of Scripture who feel a political and social obligation to this world but are gun-shy about simply reacting to what is going on. They want their political activism to be built upon a thoughtful and biblical foundation. I do not pretend to address all the issues Christians must face as they grapple with their public responsibility. But I do hope to sketch an outline for thinking and behavior that will prove helpful.

We often make the mistake of running to God for answers before we have allowed him to teach us how best to frame our questions. We come with our wrongheaded agenda when what we need is a radical transformation of perspective. As a protection against this tendency, I have written (for the most part) expositionally rather than topically. We want to be patient rather than impatient children—gathering quietly in the Father's study to hear him out, rather than dragging him by the hand to and from the rooms of our choosing. Chapter one studies the reign of God as set forth in Psalm 97. Chapter two endeavors to clarify, on the basis of the Great Commission and 1 Timothy 2:1-6, the priorities of the church (as distinguished from those of individual Christians) in public life. Chapter three considers the meaning of the apostle Peter's claim that we are "aliens and strangers." Chapters four, five, and six explore the ramifications of Jesus' remarkable command in Mark 12:17 to "give to Caesar what is Caesar's and to God what is God's." The final two chapters explore a series of principles for effecting social and political change.

At the end of each chapter you will find some questions whose purpose is to help you explore and apply the ideas of the chapter more deeply. You may want to tackle them on your own, but you would do better, it seems to me, to discuss them with a group of friends, fellow students, or colleagues.

I include two documents in the appendices. The first is the

Williamsburg Charter, drafted at the time of our Constitution's bicentennial to celebrate and reaffirm the meaning of religious freedom in our pluralistic day. Signed by a broad spectrum of Americans, the charter has helped me immensely as I have wrestled with the issues addressed in this book. The second, titled "Christian Citizenship," contains the text of a brochure we developed and routinely distributed at Three Village Church, a parish in which I served for twelve years. I offer it as an example of the sort of guidance churches should be giving to their people and as an inducement to produce better ones.

Thanks are due to Charles Colson, whose *Kingdoms in Conflict* motivated and enlightened me. Those who are aware of the work of Os Guinness, James Hunter, and John Seel will recognize their influence as well. I am particularly grateful to the elders and members of Three Village Church, who kindly granted the sabbatical that made this project possible.

Charles Drew
Setauket, New York

PSALM 97

The LORD reigns, let the earth be glad;
   let the distant shores rejoice.

Clouds and thick darkness surround him;
   righteousness and justice are the foundation of his
   throne.
Fire goes before him
   and consumes his foes on every side.
His lightning lights up the world;
   the earth sees and trembles.
The mountains melt like wax before the LORD,
   before the LORD of all the earth.
The heavens proclaim his righteousness,
   and all the peoples see his glory.
All who worship images are put to shame,
      those who boast in idols—
   worship him, all you gods!

Zion hears and rejoices
   and the villages of Judah are glad
   because of your judgments, O LORD.
For you, O LORD, are the Most High over all the earth;
   you are exalted far above all gods.

Let those who love the LORD hate evil,
   for he guards the lives of his faithful ones
   and delivers them from the hand of the wicked.
Light is shed upon the righteous
   and joy on the upright in heart.
Rejoice in the LORD, you who are righteous,
   and praise his holy name.

Chapter One

FIRST
PRINCIPLES

SOME MEMBERS OF MY CONGREGATION REJOICED AT THE RESULTS OF the 1994 elections. They saw the Republican triumph as a harbinger of moral, fiscal, and educational renewal. Others were less sanguine, pointing to the new guard's positions on gun control and the environment, for example, as huge moral blind spots. I remained skeptical because I did not see the sort of grassroots repentance without which political change means very little in the long run. In any case, few disputed the continued presence in our culture of deep, often violently polarizing differences of conviction over a wide range of issues. The bombing of the Murrah Federal Building in Oklahoma City, coming as it did after the '94 elections, checked our optimism somewhat.

The worriers among us found plenty of things to worry about. The interest on the national debt defied calculation. The Social Security system promised to place an impossible load on our children. Lethal violence in our cities, committed with alarming frequency and indifference by the young, continued to rise. Schools were so beset by unruly students and uncertain standards that they seemed unable either to educate or to develop character.

Sometime later, at the threshold of the new millennium, things looked a bit less gloomy. Francis Fukuyama pointed to drops in crime, teenage pregnancy, divorce, welfare load, and illiteracy, and to a general rise in confidence in the federal government.[1]

Despite the end-of-the-millennium upturn, nationwide disagreements, some very deep, will not disappear. My suspicion is that the remarkably strong economy in the late nineties masked, but did not end, the culture wars.

How do we tackle the inevitable problems of a society when we disagree deeply on so many basic issues? Unable to talk constructively about our differences amid rising pluralism, we tend to drift toward a politics shorn of everything but power. Social commentators have maintained that the politics of power, enhanced by the media's sound-bite approach to issues, leaves little room for human respect and for the old arts of persuasion and serious debate—qualities without which genuine democracy suffers in an atmosphere of anger, suspicion, fear, and even violence.[2] We may be closer than we care to think (imagine American social life if the stock market were seriously to crash) to the sort of tragedy that erupted throughout the Balkans in the 1990s, a dark suggestion recently made by Czech Republic president Václav Havel:

> The unnatural bipolar system imposed upon the world, which concealed or directly suppressed historical differences, has collapsed. And these differences are now manifesting themselves with sudden and nearly explosive force, not just in the post-Communist world but also in the West and many other areas of the globe. I fully agree with those who see in this reality the seeds of one of the most serious threats to humanity in the coming era.[3]

Those who find President Havel unduly pessimistic, at least with respect to the United States, might consider the resurgence of racial supremacy movements, some of whose leaders see violence as a legitimate form of political protest. Christians who feel marginalized in the battle against the things that trouble them—notably secularization, media violence and promiscuity, family decay, failures in education, intrusive government, and abortion—can be drawn into such movements.

What can feed Christians' distress even more is that, when things heat up in society, they often begin fighting with each other. I have friends whose church body exploded recently over whether or not the Lord prefers us to educate our children by home schooling. How can we be salt and light in our confused culture when we ourselves cannot agree, or when we cannot disagree amicably?

Don't Panic

Psalm 97 sets forth what we might call "first principles for the Christian citizen." The first of these "first principles" is that Christians need never panic, since our God rules everything: "The LORD reigns, let the earth be glad; let the distant shores rejoice." "Reigns" is a political word. It describes a king exercising dominion over his subjects, the ancient equivalent (roughly) of saying, "President So-and-So sits in the Oval Office." Of course, verse 1 says much more. We elect American presidents for a brief time. Their "reign" is neither permanent nor absolute nor flawless nor worldwide, whereas our God's is all four. His rule causes the "*earth* [to] be glad" and the "*distant shores* [to] rejoice" (emphasis added). Verse 9 declares his absolute sovereignty over all authorities, whether seen or unseen: "For you, O LORD, are the Most High over all the earth; you are exalted far above all gods." What an encouragement! What a source of confidence and joy for the believer! God is in charge—absolutely.

Those who bemoan the moral and social disintegration of American culture are often right. But when they speak to us in such a way as to stir up fear and panic in our hearts, they are wrong. Our God reigns, and therefore we need not—we must not—be afraid as we exercise our civic responsibilities, no matter what seems to be going on around us.

Consider the damage panic can bring. First of all, panic impairs judgment. If we give in to the voice that cries, "Act now, or our great country will be forever lost!" we will find ourselves demanding quick and easy solutions to our nation's problems, when in fact there are no such solutions. Christians, more than any others, should know that no candidate, no platform, no party has all the answers. But fear makes it easy to forget this.

Panic breeds impatience not only with political process but also with people. It easily leads to browbeating and to polarization even in the church—the very place where God expects us to model the one community that will outlast all others. How quickly and tragically we accuse and demonize one another when we are afraid. Our hearts break over the killing of millions of unborn children, but are we really right to label every pro-choicer an advocate of murder, and every woman who submits to abortion an accomplice in murder? What of the young woman who has been persuaded that the child within is not yet a child?[4] What of the person who votes pro-choice because she cannot see how the legal battle against abortion will succeed rather than because she is pro-abortion? Because panic cries, "Do something right now, before it is too late!" it dehumanizes us in our dealings with each other. For me to understand my neighbor's motives and reasoning takes time—the very thing panic cannot stand.

Panic also displeases God. Fear is a matter of the heart, and our King cares deeply and especially about our hearts, since it is from them that everything else issues (see Matthew 12:33-37; Mark 7:20-23). God cares about *why* we do something at least as much as he cares about *what* we do. Psalm 97 reminds us that, deep down, the fundamental tone of our lives must be joyful confidence in God's sovereign reign, not fear: "The LORD reigns, let the earth *be glad*; let the distant shores *rejoice*. . . . *Rejoice* in the LORD, you who are righteous, and *praise* his holy name" (verses 1,12, emphasis added). When I choose political and social action because I am afraid, even if I can justify that action from Scripture, I am denying God at a deep level. I am acting from unbelief. I am taking his majestic name in vain.

The next time you find yourself driven by fear, or you hear a message that urges you to act out of fear, consider Jesus. Our Lord saw the desperate evils of life far more clearly than we ever will, and yet he never panicked. In *The Waiting Father* Helmut Thielicke wrote:

> What tremendous pressures there must have been within him to drive him to hectic, nervous, explosive activity! He sees . . . as no one else ever sees, with an infinite and awful nearness . . . the agony of the dying man, the prisoner's torment, the anguish of the wounded conscience, injustice, terror, dread, and beastliness. . . . Must he not begin immediately to set the fire burning, to win people, to work out strategic plans . . . to work . . . furiously . . . before the night comes when no man can work? That's what we would imagine the earthly life of the Son of God to be like, if we were to think of him in human terms. . . . But how utterly different was the actual life of Jesus! Though the burden of the whole world lay heavy on his shoulders . . . he has time to stop and talk to the individual. . . . By being obedient in his little corner of the highly provincial precincts of Nazareth and Bethlehem he allows himself to be fitted into a great mosaic whose master is God. . . . And that . . . is why peace and not unrest goes out from him. For God's faithfulness already spans the world like a rainbow: he does not need to build it; he needs only to walk beneath it.[5]

Seek God's Glory First

Psalm 97 calls us to exalt a sovereign whose reigning glory knows no national bounds. And this gives us our second "first principle": our political activism must always serve God's glory worldwide. In other words, model Christian Americans, like their counterparts in Brazil or Korea or wherever, set their hearts first and always on the promotion of God's interests.

In the classic film *Chariots of Fire*, runner Eric Liddell vividly models this priority. When the Prince of Wales and a number of other powerful figures press him to overturn his conscience-bound decision not to run on the Lord's Day, he politely refuses. A singularly obnoxious figure accuses him of arrogant disloyalty, saying, "In my day it was country first, then God." Eric fires back, "It is you who are arrogant! God made kings. God knows I love my country, but I cannot for the sake of that country do what God forbids."

Consider carefully the language of Psalm 97. Verse 1 does not read, "The Lord reigns; let America be glad!" Nor does it read, "The Lord reigns; let my family be glad!" These groups must surely join the chorus, but the choir in view is far more grand: "Let *the earth* be glad; let the *distant shores* rejoice" (emphasis added). Verses 6 and 7 convey the same idea: "The heavens proclaim his righteousness, and *all the peoples* see his glory. *All* who worship images are put to shame, those who boast in idols—worship him, *all* you gods!" (emphasis added).[6]

God's glory, the revealing and acknowledgment worldwide of who he is, what he has done, what he is doing, and what he will do—this great purpose drives history. Each nation's saga belongs to this larger one. The history of the United States, so full of God's blessing and goodness, is not for that reason a special history unto itself. It belongs, together with the histories of Peru, Estonia, China, and Senegal, to *his* story.

America and the Kingdom of God

We can draw at least one implication from this second great principle. Our deepest longing as we consider the future of America must not be that our country will be happy or peaceful or prosperous or even good. Our most fundamental goal must not be that America as we have known it (or as we imagine it to have been) will survive. We must recall that God is glorified not only in his mercies but also in his judgments.

Romans 1:18-32 describes the social and moral disintegration of an ancient culture, a disintegration disturbingly parallel to what we observe in our own country today. Paul says that this tragedy did not happen by chance but was the work of God aimed at making known his holy anger: "The wrath of God is being revealed from heaven against all the godlessness and wickedness of men who suppress the truth by their wickedness" (verse 18). Like Jeremiah and many of the prophets, the Christian must be prepared to say with tears, "Lord, if you choose (and I hope you do not) to glorify yourself in the failure of our thankless and decadent society, then so be it. Honor your name!" Our first love must not be the preservation of America as we remember it to have been, but the revelation and exaltation of the name of God in whatever ways he sees fit.

We must embrace this difficult truth or we will blind ourselves to things about our country, past and present, Republican and Democrat, that have not pleased God. We must love our country, but we must have lover's quarrels with it (starting with the citizens we know the best—ourselves), for our citizenship is in heaven.

Imagine a world without the United States. An unsettling thought, as unwelcome and as unlikely as the end of their empire would have sounded to Roman citizens at the time of Constantine. But history and Scripture teach us that nations come and go, and there is no guarantee that America will exist forever. Our duration and stability are in fact anomalies in the saga of human civilization. All human governments will one day fail, and for that reason Christians set their deepest allegiance on the glory of God's reign, not the survival of their country.

Hate Evil

We come now to a third "first principle" for civic life drawn from Psalm 97: Christians must hate evil. Abundant evidence for this principle occurs in the psalm: "Clouds and thick darkness surround him; righteousness and justice are the foundation of his throne. . . . Let those who love the LORD *hate evil,* for he guards the lives of his faithful ones and delivers them from the hand of the wicked" (verses 2,10, emphasis added). "Clouds and thick darkness" surround God's throne because he is morally unapproachable. That is, he is absolutely holy and we are not. When we read that his throne rests on "righteousness and justice," we learn that every act of his sovereign rule arises from a character and policy that are good and fair. Because of who he is, God will neither act unrighteously nor tolerate anything unrighteous throughout his dominion.

This great truth is for us a double-edged sword. On the one hand, it comforts us to know that the God who reigns over everything is good. We can know that all that is right and true and lovely will one day be gloriously vindicated. On the other hand, this truth reminds us that God is on our side only as we are on his: "Rejoice in the LORD, *you who are righteous*" (verse 12, emphasis added). Even in our most christianized moments,[7] we as a nation have never enjoyed the special relationship to God that ancient Israel enjoyed. Israel was a theocracy, the kingdom of God located in a human kingdom—something we have never been, despite the rhetoric of some, going back to colonial times.[8] And yet, for all its privileged status, not even Israel survived the righteous judgment of God when it turned from him. Patient and forgiving for many years, he nevertheless chastened his people, even to the point of exile. If Israel, which enjoyed "most favored nation" status with God, was punished for sin, can we expect an exemption?

Turning from Idols: Statism and Privatism

The most immediate and perhaps the best thing any of us could do for America, according to Psalm 97, is to search our lives and attitudes carefully and repent of our complicity in the evils of our time: "All who worship images are put to shame, those who boast in idols" (verse 7). We complain about the violence and sex in the media, and yet we belong to a culture that provides a market for that material. More to the point, we may watch more of it than we should. Many other idols dominate our attention and grip our lives—possessions, power, status, clothing, appearance, youth-fulness, and sports are a few of them, evidenced by the amount of money, time, and energy we pour into them.

Two other idols affect us more than we realize. The first I will call "statism," by which I mean the tendency to rely too much on government and the political process to bring about the changes we so deeply desire. We often hear people arguing, "If we can just get this law enacted. . . ." or "If we can just get this person into office and that person out of office, then things will be so much better." Certainly leaders and policies make some difference—Proverbs speaks of the blessings of good leaders and the curses of bad leaders—but not as much as we sometimes think, given our sprawling and bureaucratic polity. How easily (and unfairly) we tend to blame elected officials for the social ills of our time, as if greed, family problems, failures in education, inner-city violence, and the like were simply the government's fault. Those in office bear responsibility, and their decisions affect our lives to some degree, but such scapegoating (which appears with a vengeance during election years) reflects an unrealistic and idolatrous reliance upon the machinery of government.

The idol of statism appears, it seems to me, in the recent renewal by the political right of the "stealth politics" employed by the political left in the 1970s. Stealth politics, usually employed at the local level, involves promoting new and unknown people with hidden agendas. Only after their election, to the school board, for example, do they bring out the Bible and declare themselves for school prayer. The use of such questionable means for an allegedly good end dishonors the cause of God's kingdom in the community. It seems to be driven by the mistaken (and idolatrous) statist notion that runs this way: "If we can just get our people in positions of power, we will make the country a better place." Community life must be built, not imposed, as the self-invited "guests" at the Boston Tea Party reminded King George. Christians understand that both means and ends matter to God and that they err when they try to hasten his reign through deceitfully grabbing after worldly power.

Bad as it is, statism is not the only idol drawing us into complicity with the evils of our time. "Privatism" is another such idol. It influences us even more than statism, showing its influence in numerous ways. We worship privatism, for example, when we object to or are embarrassed by religious discussion in public forums. Privatists object:

"How dare you talk about God in Boy Scouts!"

"How dare you continue as a legitimate club on the grounds of this public university while holding a policy that bars practicing homosexuals from serving as officers in your group."

"How dare you try to block loving, committed couples of the same sex from solemnizing their relationship in marriage!"

"How dare you hold a Bible discussion on school grounds during school hours!"[9]

Privatists cite such behavior with disapproval as an unconstitutional breach of Thomas Jefferson's "wall of separation" between church and state.[10]

The worship of privacy lies behind these complaints. Religious truth has come to be viewed as *private* truth, and though such truth (like private property) is sacred and inviolable, it is nevertheless private. "You may believe anything you please," intones the idol of privatism, "as long as you keep it to yourself." If I publicly articulate my faith — if I discuss religious conviction in school, seek to persuade in that setting, or bring my convictions to bear upon those who may lead the social organization to which I belong — then I "go public" with something that ought to remain private. Worse, I trespass on others' private convictions. Privatism cries out, "This must not be tolerated!"

Os Guinness has observed that much of American spirituality is "personally engaging but socially irrelevant." This description sadly describes my spirituality as it does so often that of many of my Christian friends. Church, family, work, and leisure (all private concerns) tend to consume most of our attention. But this is wrong. God has placed us in this world, and he intends for us to bring glory to him by exerting all the influence we can in a spirit of love to make it a better place. It is rarely easy to do this, but it is necessary. We should keep up with civic life at every level (local, national, and international), seek to understand it, and involve ourselves in it regularly in some fashion. We are stewards of our world. God will hold us accountable.

Practicing the Golden Rule

Privatism often deeply influences even the activists among us. Many believers have sought, for example, to redress the anti-Christian bias in textbooks, to make public school facilities available after hours for Christian meetings, or to pursue litigation in defense of Christian conscience. These are all worthy undertakings, as far as they go. If Christians do not blow the whistle on such biases, who will?

The difficulty, as I see it, is that we do not go far enough. We seem to have forgotten the Golden Rule as it applies to freedom of conscience in American public life. Our interest in public life seems to extend only so far as we have felt our rights and freedoms as Christians being threatened. Would a believer who has chosen to advocate prayer in the public schools do so with the same zeal in Hawaii (where praying would as likely be to Buddha as to Christ) as in Memphis (a heavily christianized part of our country)? Perhaps not. Sadly, in our valid concern over the decay of faith in our society, we may find ourselves advocating action that marginalizes the faith of the lonely Jewish kid in the otherwise Christian fourth-grade classroom in rural Mississippi.

Do you see the problem? Christians are, or appear to be, religiously self-serving when it comes to their engagement with public life. We can so easily forget that freedom of conscience—of *every* conscience—is a Christian principle worth dying for.[11] In a day when so many angrily assert their rights, Christians have a remarkable opportunity to demonstrate a totally different mind-set, the mind-set of a statesman—one that firmly defends the nonChristian's right to believe as he or she does.

Christian statesmen are the best sort of activists. Like other activists, they bring their convictions to bear on public life. But they go a step further. Committed to the God-given dignity of every person, they defend the right of their nonChristian neighbor to bring his or her convictions to bear on public life, even when they heartily disagree with those convictions. They say in effect, "I think you are dead wrong in what you believe, but I will go to the wall for your freedom to argue for it."[12]

Can you imagine the American Civil Liberties Union and the Christian Legal Society working together on anything? Many American Christians find the notion difficult to swallow, but they should not if they understand what we are saying here about Christian statesmanship. Christian statesmen love their neighbor as themselves, and are therefore at least as ready to keep the government from bearing down on an atheist for his or her "faith" as they are to keep the government from bearing down on Christians for theirs. They will see as equally worthy of legal consideration the rights of a Caribbean cult to sacrifice chickens in Miami and the rights of a fundamentalist church in rural Ohio to start a school. With a love undergirded by confidence in Christ's ability to promote his kingdom in any setting, they resist the temptation to be privacy-driven religious reactionaries, concerned only to defend their turf from their enemies. They always have an eye on the common good.

Sadly, Christian activists tend to forget that if we do not defend religious freedom generally, if we are not deeply concerned for Christ's sake in the defense of *all* religious freedom, then in the end we will lose our own. We undermine our own freedom when the only agenda we bring to politics is a selfish one.

MAKING IT PERSONAL

1. What social issues would you rather not talk about at church or with a friend? Why?
2. Consider the following statement by Czech president Václav Havel. Do you agree with his analysis of the post-Communist world? Why or why not?

    The unnatural bipolar system imposed upon the world, which concealed or directly suppressed historical differences, has collapsed. And these differences are now manifesting themselves with sudden and nearly explosive force, not just in the post-Communist world but also in the West and many other areas of the globe. I fully agree with those who see in this reality the seeds of one of the most serious threats to humanity in the coming era.

3. The first "first principle for the Christian citizen" is *don't panic*. What are you most fearful of as you contemplate the American political and social scene? According to Psalm 97, why is your worry inappropriate and what damage can it lead to?

4. The second "first principle" is *seek God's glory first*. Read Romans 1:18-32, which reminds us that God is glorified in judgment just as he is in mercy. Where do you see God's mercy at work in American society? Where do you see his judgment?

5. The third "first principle" is *hate evil*. In your own words, what are the idols of "statism" and "privatism" as described in this chapter? How might you, your family, or your church be seduced by them?

6. In December 1999 the United States Supreme Court agreed to hear a case involving a dispute over whether students at a Texas high school should be permitted to continue their long-standing practice of praying over the stadium P.A. system just before kickoff at football games. If you were a member of the Supreme Court, how would you rule, particularly in light of the observation in this chapter that "our interest in public life seems to extend only so far as we have felt our rights and freedoms as Christians being threatened"?

MATTHEW 28:16-20

Then the eleven disciples went to Galilee, to the mountain where Jesus had told them to go. When they saw him, they worshiped him; but some doubted. Then Jesus came to them and said, "All authority in heaven and on earth has been given to me. Therefore go and make disciples of all nations, baptizing them in the name of the Father and of the Son and of the Holy Spirit, and teaching them to obey everything I have commanded you. And surely I am with you always, to the very end of the age."

1 TIMOTHY 2:1-6

I urge . . . , first of all, that requests, prayers, intercession and thanksgiving be made for everyone—for kings and all those in authority, that we may live peaceful and quiet lives in all godliness and holiness. This is good, and pleases God our Savior, who wants all men to be saved and to come to a knowledge of the truth. For there is one God and one mediator between God and men, the man Christ Jesus, who gave himself as a ransom for all men.

Chapter Two

KEEPING THE CHURCH FOCUSED

MOST FIRST-GRADE CLASSROOMS HAVE AT LEAST ONE TOMMY THE Terrible. We can picture him standing defiantly on his desk. His teacher tells him to sit, but he shakes his head.

"Tommy, if you do not sit down right away, I will have to come over there and make you sit."

"You can't make me do nothin'!"

The teacher walks over to Tommy's desk, picks him up, and forces him into his seat.

"There now, Tommy, you *are* sitting down."

To which Tommy replies defiantly, "I may be sittin' down on the outside, but I'm standin' up on the inside!"

Societies change most dramatically as people change, one by one, from the inside out, rather than by the imposition of rules and restraints from the outside in or from the top down. Sometimes, of course, those restraints must be imposed. That is why God established government—and the schoolteacher! They are institutions without which people's natural selfishness would reign uncontrollably and make living together impossible. But a greater glory shines, and a better society thrives, when people voluntarily come to bow with joy before the King of kings and this heartfelt allegiance spills over into all of life. Renewed by the indwelling Holy Spirit, who writes God's moral law on the heart (see Ezekiel 36:25-28), people need less and less the fear of governmental sanctions to make them live as they should.

Who is responsible for advancing this powerful and strategic solution to society's woes? Clearly, it is the church. After all, if the church does not tell people about the life-changing Christ and does not pray for that message to penetrate, who will? This is the church's primary calling, a calling that should caution believers against pouring the church's energies unduly into politics. Whatever we do individually in our efforts to honor the King socially, we must hold the church to Jesus' mandate in Matthew 28.

Diversions and Divisions

Politics in the church can divert it from its strategic calling. When the hot social issues of the day drive the church's teaching and activity, they drain it of vital energy that ought to be used elsewhere. I remember working once with a church task force seeking to come up with guidelines on what sorts of political publications should be made available, and how they should be made available, at the church. It took months, and we never implemented the unwieldy results of our effort. I completed the undertaking with a strong sense that we would have done better to have given our efforts to other matters.

Politics in the church also compromises its primary task by dividing people along nonessential lines. This division can take at least two forms. First, it divides church people from each other. Politics is a very imperfect science—the important but fallible efforts of fallible people to make life in our fallen world better, according to fallible and limited understanding. Because of its imperfections, politics will without fail divide good Christian people from each other as they seek to follow their own consciences, wrestling with the complexity of social and political life.

Such differences are not inherently bad; they can reflect the rich diversity of gifts and callings that exist in the body of Christ. But they can split a church if the church begins to endorse one strategy or calling at the expense of another.

Politics can also divide people from the church—a serious problem indeed. Imagine someone visiting your church next Sunday. She has not been to church in years and is coming because of a providential crisis that has opened her heart to God. Imagine furthermore that she is a staunch Republican, whose parents and grandparents were all highly involved in Republican politics, and who is herself quite active in local party efforts. Imagine, finally, that as she walks in the door of the church, someone hands her a leaflet that "smells" pro-Democrat. It does not say, "Vote for 'So-and-So.'" But by the way it is formatted, by the issues that it lists and by the issues that it does not list, our visitor knows that Democrats wrote it. What will she do? She may be desperate enough spiritually to stick around and listen to the preacher. On the other hand, she might turn around without a word and leave, saying to herself, *I did not come here to be a Democrat.* Should the church run this risk—not for its sake, but for hers?[1]

Certainly the church does not exist to please people. Jesus said, "I did not come to bring peace, but a sword" (Matthew 10:34). Neither the law of God, which exposes our sin, nor his cross, which offends our self-righteousness, makes people comfortable. But the church must take care that the law and the gospel, and not something else, do the dividing. Our primary concern—concern for the glory of God in the transformation of people through the gospel—should lead us in our corporate life to be a place where people from varied political backgrounds, convinced of varied political strategies, feel socially and politically safe. We must be a place where one's politics do not make him or her a second-class citizen, but rather a place where we can agree to disagree in the spirit of loving dialogue.

Praying Down the Kingdom

In the midst of giving a commencement address, a speaker began by asking everyone to rise. He then said: "Those of you who do not know the name of your state governor, please sit and remain seated." Some sat down. Then he said, "Those of you who do not know the name of at least one of your state's senators in Washington, please sit." A larger number took their seats. He continued, "Those of you who do not know the names of *both* your state's senators, please sit." Lots of people sat down. He next asked, "Those of you who do not know the names of your district representatives in your state government, please sit." By that time, all but a handful were off their feet. Then the speaker observed, "Friends, if we do not know the names of these people, how can we be praying for them?"

Perhaps more than any other prophet, Daniel was privileged to see the hand of God behind human history. On one occasion, after a vision had driven him to three weeks of fasting and prayer, a glorious and terrifying figure visited him and said:

> Do not be afraid, Daniel. Since the first day that you set
> your mind to gain understanding and to humble yourself
> before your God, your words were heard, and I have come
> in response to them. But the prince of the Persian king-
> dom resisted me twenty-one days. Then Michael, one of
> the chief princes, came to help me, because I was
> detained there with the king of Persia. Now I have come
> to explain to you what will happen to your people in the
> future. (Daniel 10:12-14)

These words remind us that national and international developments are in some mysterious fashion linked to angelic conflict in a world we cannot see. They remind us, furthermore, that when we pray for the nations, we lift ourselves into this great conflict.

There is tremendous political power in prayer, especially now that Jesus has ascended "far above all rule and authority, power and dominion." God has "placed all things under his feet and appointed him to be head over everything *for the church*" (Ephesians 1:21-22, emphasis added). This means that we have influence over every government on earth, simply by prayer.

The wonderful thing about political praying is that it is a form of "power politics" open to all. Anyone can do it: the shut-in who can't get out to the polling station, the twelve-year-old who is not old enough to vote, the conscientious citizen who has studied an issue carefully and is still confused about it, the civil servant who is dismayed by the corruption and inefficiency in the department where he works, the soldier on the battlefield, the official in the State Department struggling with how best to respond to an international crisis, the missionary who is being thrown out of an Islamic nation whose government has just turned radical, the national believer who is on trial for her faith, the young black who is pulled over on the highway for racial reasons.

How Do We Pray?
Pray we can and pray we must. But how should we pray? What comes after "God bless and keep America"? Is this even the right way to pray? Paul gives us helpful counsel in 1 Timothy 2:1-6:

> I urge . . . , first of all, that requests, prayers, interces-
> sion and thanksgiving be made for everyone—for kings
> and all those in authority, that we may live peaceful
> and quiet lives in all godliness and holiness. This is
> good, and pleases God our Savior, who wants all men
> to be saved and to come to a knowledge of the truth.
> For there is one God and one mediator between God
> and men, the man Christ Jesus, who gave himself as a
> ransom for all men.

Note first off that our praying must be international. "God bless America" is fine, but it is not enough. Paul commands us to intercede and give thanks "for kings and all those in authority." The world political scene must be on our hearts as we pray. The Bible sets the agenda for prayer, and the evening news fills in the details. It would do our world great good if God's people read the *New York Times* on their knees!

We should pray "thanksgiving," not simply "requests" and "intercessions." It is remarkable that Paul would counsel thanksgiving in the world he knew, a place of political despotism! But he did, perhaps partly because the fragile church was often wrongfully accused of revolutionary aims and needed for its survival to show its good intentions. But surely Paul had other reasons. He saw government as God's gracious way of controlling the socially destructive impact of sin. He also had the wisdom to see that for all its imperfections, the Roman rule brought the sort of order and stability that made mission work and evangelism possible. As biblical historian E. J. Goodspeed said, "It was the glory of the Roman Empire that it brought peace to a troubled world. Under its sway the regions of Asia Minor and the East enjoyed tranquility and security to an extent and for a length of time unknown before and probably since. It was the 'Pax Romana.'"[2]

Pollsters tell us that many Americans are bitter and cynical about their political leaders today. It leads me to imagine that if any praying gets done at all, its tone is frustrated and its content is judgmental: "Lord, change that man or get rid of him! Lord, send an old-fashioned firestorm on those self-serving bureaucrats!" We err when we pray this way. It makes the already difficult task of governing in our age even more difficult. Many in our government work very hard at doing what they genuinely feel is best in settings that invariably require compromise and that invariably draw flak. Many of the best-qualified people never even enter politics because it is so thankless and difficult.

Those who govern us need our encouragement at least as much as our criticism. When we thank God for our leaders, when we call to mind in prayer the good things they do and the efforts they make, we find ourselves behaving more charitably toward them. This change in us fosters a climate in which they find it easier to govern more responsibly. By contrast, negative praying tends to feed the cynicism we are naturally prone to, and cynicism discourages our leaders.

Such a dynamic may be more difficult to envision in national politics than at a local level (we are far more likely to rub shoulders with the members of our district's school board than we are with our state's senators). But I believe that it can happen at any level. Do not underestimate the power of attitude. It cannot be legislated, but it is often more powerful than any law.

According to the apostle, the aim of our prayers for world leaders should be "that we may lead peaceful and quiet lives in all godliness and holiness." He envisions the maintenance of the kind of national peace and stability that will enable godliness and reverence to flourish openly. And we should desire this, he says, because God "wants all men to be saved" through the "one mediator between God and men, the man Christ Jesus." In other words, we should pray earnestly for the nations of the world, that their leaders will establish the sort of peace in which Jesus Christ can be promoted without hindrance. And we must pray this way so that the one true God's international kingdom may be built.

With the collapse of Soviet Russia we rightly rejoiced before God at the end of a godless regime that often oppressed both human freedom generally and Christian proclamation particularly. Where we may have been politically shortsighted and theologically mistaken was in the assumption that this collapse somehow proved that what God really wants everywhere in the world is Western-style democracy and market capitalism. Paul tells us that God longs for "all men . . . to come to a knowledge of the truth." We must take seriously the possibility that the imposition of

America's political and economic traditions wholesale on a different culture (whether it is Russia or Haiti or any other country) may *not* be God's will, particularly if it causes such political distress as to shut down Christian testimony entirely. And such a shutdown can happen if that testimony is linked to an American "takeover."

How did you pray during Operation Desert Storm? I suspect you prayed for our soldiers, for their safety, perhaps even for their spiritual well-being and for the effective ministry of military chaplains (war often brings people face-to-face with the Lord). I remember praying earnestly for a rapid end to the hostilities and for minimal loss of life. Certainly it was right to pray for these things; if we didn't pray for our troops, who would?

But Paul, I believe, would have had us pray for more. He would have had us pray for the Iraqi soldiers, for the people of Iraq and Kuwait and Israel, for Saddam Hussein and the other political and military leaders in the region. Paul would have reminded us that there is something far worse than an oil shortage, than America losing face, than bloodshed, even than the collapse of Iraqi sanitation, health care, and food distribution. He would have reminded us that worse than any of these things is the destiny of any—whether American, Jew, or Arab—who perishes without knowing the living God through his appointed mediator. Paul would no doubt have pointed to the spiritual darkness of Islam, to its grip upon millions, and urged us to pray that God's people, however few they may be among the Muslim peoples, would be given freedom to live out the gospel in word and deed. And Paul would especially have urged us to pray that somehow the people of Iraq would not be given the impression that *Christian* America was their enemy. For to have linked the United States with the Christian God, a linkage that sadly many Americans came close to making during that war, would have been to declare that an Iraqi citizen would commit treason if he or she ever converted to Jesus Christ.

How did you pray during NATO's conflict with Yugoslavia?

I suspect you prayed for a quick ending both to the bombing and to Milosevic's ruthless policy of ethnic cleansing. You probably prayed, as I did, for the safety of the pilots, for the safety of non-combatants, and for justice. But did you also pray for the Serbian church? Perhaps the greatest evil of all was the complicity of those who called themselves Christians in the rape and pillage of their Muslim neighbors. How could the loving reign of God's one true mediator possibly be advanced under such circumstances? Paul would have had us pray for the Serbian church and its leaders, that by their teaching, example, and prayer they would subvert the centuries-old hatred in the region and exalt the Prince of Peace. He would have had us pray similarly for all believers and their leaders, not just Serbian, but ethnic Albanian and NATO-affiliated. He would have had us pray for political and military leaders (Christian and nonChristian), that by their policies, words, and attitudes they would restrain vengeance and advance the sort of peace that would enable God's people to represent him freely by word and deed.

Staying on Track

We must take care, as God's people, to stay on track. We must protect the church in its high and specific calling, and resist the ever-present temptation to draw it as an institution into the important but short-term solutions of politics. We must also pray for the whole world, remembering as we do so that the God we love is neither an American nor a capitalist, and that he has managed quite ably through centuries of monarchs and despots to save his people, to train them, and to use them in the forward march of his kingdom.

MAKING IT PERSONAL

1. Have you ever seen politics divert or divide a church? Describe and analyze what happened. What lessons, if any, did you learn?

2. Take a personal inventory of your "political" prayer life. Do you know the names of all the public officials who serve you? Do you know their spouses' names? Do you know the issues they are grappling with? How often in the past month have you prayed for them? Have you given thanks for their service? How often in the past month have you prayed for a foreign government's officials and policies?

3. Describe your attitude toward politics and politicians. Is it cynical, hopeful, utopian, or something else? Why do you hold your particular attitude? Measure it against what you imagine Jesus' attitude would be. What steps can you take to improve your attitude?

4. Carefully read over 1 Timothy 2:1-6 and then use it as a springboard to pray for a particular nation or continent. As you do so, bear in mind the following summary of Paul's advice on page 25: "We should pray earnestly for the nations of the world, that their leaders will establish the sort of peace in which Jesus Christ can be promoted without hindrance. And we must pray this way so that the one true God's international kingdom may be built."

1 PETER 2:11-17

Dear friends, I urge you, as aliens and strangers in the world, to abstain from sinful desires, which wage war against your soul. Live such good lives among the pagans that, though they accuse you of doing wrong, they may see your good deeds and glorify God on the day he visits us.

Submit yourselves for the Lord's sake to every authority instituted among men: whether to the king, as the supreme authority, or to governors, who are sent by him to punish those who do wrong and to commend those who do right. For it is God's will that by doing good you should silence the ignorant talk of foolish men. Live as free men, but do not use your freedom as a cover-up for evil; live as servants of God. Show proper respect to everyone: Love the brotherhood of believers, fear God, honor the king.

Chapter Three

EXEMPLARY
AMBASSADORS

I GREW UP ON THE NORTH SHORE OF LONG ISLAND, SPENDING MY
summers as a child at a local yacht club, where I learned to sail
and where, as I got older, I found summer employment. One of
the most coveted jobs at the club was launch driving. Launch-
boys operated the twenty-five-foot inboard yacht tenders that
took boaters to and from their vessels. The launches were fun to
drive, the job paid very well (tips supplemented an already good
salary), and the social life was enviable (one could usually get
away with ferrying lady friends around the fleet).

The job required a Coast Guard license, for which one had
to be eighteen and pass an extensive written test. When I was
old enough, I applied for the job and to my great delight was
accepted, provided I could obtain the license. To my dismay,
I discovered that before I could even sit for the test I had to
document that I had spent at least two hundred hours as a
launch-boy trainee—something I had never done. I brought the
matter up with my employer, mentioning that I had never heard
of any such program at the yacht club. He chuckled and said
that, knowing my substantial experience around boats, he would

happily testify in writing that I had the required training. This made sense because the apparent intent of the Coast Guard's stipulation was to assure that launch drivers were "water wise," so I agreed.

That night, however, I couldn't sleep. I desperately wanted the job, but I could not in good conscience be a party to a deliberate deception. After a long struggle, I decided to approach my boss and tell him that I would rather submit to the Coast Guard a summary of my actual boating experience and ask them to accept this in lieu of the training. He couldn't understand why I wanted to do this, remarking that I was clearly experienced enough and that his standard practice had always been to indicate that the training had taken place. Since he kept pressing me for an explanation, I finally took a deep breath and told him that I had to go this route because I was a Christian. Fearful that he might dismiss me altogether as a fanatic or as a "holier than thou" type sitting in judgment upon his customary practice, I had wanted to avoid this explanation, but he would not let me.

My faith and gratitude soared when he smiled and said, "Okay. Good luck." Happily, the Coast Guard accepted my experience as valid and I went on to obtain both the license and the job. My boss and I never talked further about the matter, but I hoped in retrospect that Christ used the stand I had taken in his life in some way.

This story dramatizes in a small way the interaction between faith and public life. I could not sleep because I knew that what I wanted and what my boss permitted were not the only standards by which I was to operate. I was Christ's ambassador, called to represent him in this situation, called to submit myself for his sake to every authority.

New Contexts, Same Principles

Our political experience differs, in some ways dramatically, from the experience of those to whom Peter wrote in the first century

A.D. We do not live under despotic, or even monarchic, rule. We belong to a representative democracy where we, through our elected officials, are "the king." We live in a tradition that values highly the freedoms of expression, assembly, and worship. And though the church no longer enjoys the cultural dominance it once did, neither is it the new and fragile creature it was when the apostle Peter wrote.

Despite the differences between Peter's political world and our own, many deeper truths remain constant. One, noted in the first chapter, is that our God reigns—a profoundly reassuring fact for all who love him and desire to see his justice and righteousness triumph. Another, which we will consider now, is that we have a sociopolitical identity that transcends whatever national or party alignment we may presently have taken on.

Peter calls us "aliens and strangers in the world" (1 Peter 2:11), aligning us not with the United States or the Republican Party or China but with the kingdom of heaven. If we are Christians, there is a deep sense in which we do not belong here. To use the language of the New English Bible, we are "aliens in a foreign land." We share much in common with Daniel and Esther, Jews who were uprooted from their native surroundings and obliged to live among people whose language, customs, and beliefs differed dramatically from their own. To put the matter positively, we belong most profoundly to Christ, whose reign extends far wider than the borders of the nation whose passport we carry. Paul wrote, "Our citizenship is in heaven" (Philippians 3:20; see also Colossians 1:13 and Hebrews 13:14)—a notion receiving some elaboration in the second-century *Letter to Diognetus:* "They [that is, Christians] dwell each in his native land, but only as resident aliens; they carry out all the tasks of a citizen, and endure all the burdens like foreigners; every foreign land is a native land to them, and every native land is a foreign land to them."[1]

Making the Case for the King

Living out our American citizenship in a manner that pleases God depends in large measure upon knowing and believing in this deeper identity. Remembering that we serve a King who loves us enough to have died for us gives us peace and hope regardless of America's condition. Believing that Christ welcomes us as fellow royalty in his court gives us security and a sense of place even if society marginalizes us. Knowing that Jesus' kingdom will never end arms us with patience. Recalling that our Master aims ever to broaden his dominion fires our efforts to be his worthy ambassadors.

The apostle Peter had this last implication particularly in mind: "Live such good lives among the pagans that, though they accuse you of doing wrong, they may see your good deeds and glorify God on the day he visits us. Submit yourselves for the Lord's sake to every authority. . . . For it is God's will that by doing good you should silence the ignorant talk of foolish men" (1 Peter 2:12-13,15). Peter commanded us to live exemplary public lives, and he did so primarily because he knew that by doing so we will make it difficult or impossible for people to ignore our King.

Holy Freedom

One quality of exemplary public living is what we might call holy freedom. Americans wrangle over freedom with great heat these days. At stake most of the time is a host of private freedoms— freedom to express myself sexually or artistically or religiously or politically. We tend to frame the debate largely in terms of personal rights—the right of a teacher to carry a Bible to school, the right of homosexual couples to live together and to express their affection publicly, the right of filmmakers to depict whatever they choose, the right to produce, distribute, and view pornographic material.

Christians should understand and enjoy freedom. The cross frees us from condemnation under the law. The Father's love frees us from enslavement to the opinions of people. The Holy Spirit frees us from bondage to sin. And yet, if we understand the nature of our heavenly citizenship, we will understand that we are not free to do whatever we please. Peter wrote, "Live as free men, but do not use your freedom as a cover-up for evil; live as servants of God" (verse 16). My personal freedom is not a freedom from all restraint but rather a freedom from sin and selfishness. God has set me free to serve him before a watching and antagonistic world. He has liberated me to "make the case" for his character and ways by the way I live. As Peter put it, "It is God's will that by doing good you should silence the ignorant talk of foolish men" (verse 15).

Squeaky Clean
Do you know that throughout his long career as an evangelist, Billy Graham never traveled alone? Wherever he went, he brought with him either his wife or a male traveling companion. Did you know that at the end of every crusade the Graham organization routinely commissions an independent audit of all the campaign finances and has the results printed in a major newspaper? These matters are perhaps news to you. What I suspect is not news to you are Jimmy Swaggart's and Jim Baker's sexual misconduct and the fraud and racketeering convictions of National Baptist Convention leader Henry J. Lyons.

Why do so many more Americans know so much more about the bad behavior of certain Christian leaders than they know about the good behavior of other Christian leaders? There are perhaps many secondary reasons, but the deepest reason is that the world prefers sin to righteousness. More telling, the world (incited by the Devil) hates Christ and pounces with relish upon anything that will drag down Christ's reputation or make him in some way irrelevant. The world does not want to deal with Christ and looks hard for reasons to ignore him. The apostle Peter knew this, as does the spiritually sensitive citizen of Christ's kingdom today. For this reason Peter urged us to bend over backward, for the sake of our King and out of love for others, to live public lives that are squeaky clean.

On numerous occasions I have found myself counseling Christian couples who are engaged and living together. Some are sleeping together; others are not. Rarely, in either case, has much thought been given to the reputation of Christ and the impact of appearances on a watching world. With alarming frequency, professing Christians appear in the news and in everyday life as those who seem unwilling or unable to keep promises. The divorce rate among Christian couples is barely distinguishable from the national rate.

In my experience Christians appear to be as sloppy about paying back loans as anyone. When this happens in the church, the place where we can so easily presume upon one another's generosity (all in the name of trust and love), the results are usually painful and often publicly divisive. Disregarding Paul's command, Christians take each other to court, bringing public shame upon the One who died to make them one (see 1 Corinthians 6:1-11).

My friend Don, an ardent and outspoken Christian, once ran a small business. A number of years ago it fell on hard times and he found himself owing over $50,000. Pressed by many friends to file for bankruptcy, he concluded that he could not do so without compromising his testimony. He chose rather to approach each of his creditors personally, ask for their patience, and promise to pay them back a bit at a time. They consented, and in five years he obliterated the debt. What governed Don throughout that arduous five years was a desire to see Christ honored publicly through his financial integrity.

Christians who understand their deepest citizenship are never content merely to be happy in Christ. They aim as well to be above reproach—to live a life that in every part commends their heavenly King. They always deal honestly with people. They tell the truth about themselves when asked. They keep their promises, small and great. They pay all their bills, including those that are not legally enforceable. And they pay their bills on time. Like my friend Don, they are governed by a holy fear at the thought that

Jesus Christ might cease to be an issue because of their public behavior. People differ on how deeply the press or Senate ought to be allowed to probe the personal lives of those in public office (remember "Monicagate"?). Without entering that debate, let me say that every Christian—whether seeking office or not—should be able to stand such a probe.

More Than Just Playing It Safe

Peter said that we should "live such good lives among the pagans that . . . they may . . . glorify God on the day he visits us" (1 Peter 2:12). We must aim not only at silencing "foolish men" but also at eliciting godly praise from them. This will happen only as we turn from merely avoiding questionable practices and appearances to engaging ourselves in aggressive goodness. Public apathy is no more an option for us than is public scandal.

I remember well the day some law students in my congregation came to me following a sermon on the rights of the unborn. They said, "We agree with you, but what are we to do for pregnant women who cannot or will not raise their children?" Their concern began a process that culminated in the creation of a crisis pregnancy center and a number of local shelters for unwed mothers. We must forever be asking, "How can we commend the good, just, and merciful reign of our King if we ourselves are not demonstrating it?"

On the Edge of Eternity

As I write, my office and house are in disarray. Furniture long in need of reupholstering is at the shop; our den floor (long in need of refinishing) is bare and awaiting a second coat of polyurethane; files long overdue for a purging are being purged. We have undertaken all these things at once because in four weeks we will be moving. The deadline has focused us remarkably.

None of us knows precisely when we will be "moving" to glory. What we do know is that this move is certain; it may happen at any moment, and when it does happen, the Lord will make all things right. These certainties give focus to our daily living. The apostle Peter certainly believed these things and counseled his readers, many of who were suffering in their role as ambassadors, to draw their hope from them. He reminded them of the day when their accusers would "see [their] good deeds and glorify God" (verse 12).

This may sound morbid or vindictive, and indeed it can be. But it was neither morbid nor vindictive for Peter and the apostles, whose writings resound with rejoicing and love. For them the nearness of the end gave fullness and hope to the present. It made every moment and every personal encounter (even with those who hated them) important. Knowing that the good for which I am working will certainly be vindicated gives me hope. And knowing that that vindication may come, despite appearances, before the day is over energizes that hope remarkably. Knowing that the person I am speaking with may at any moment meet God makes me eager to commend his holy love by my behavior. We can learn from the Puritans here:

> Dr. Johnson is credited with the remark that when a man knows that he is going to be hanged in a fortnight it concentrates his mind wonderfully, and in the same way the Puritans' awareness that in the midst of life we are in death . . . gave them a deep seriousness, calm yet passionate, with regard to the business of living that Christians in today's opulent, mollycoddled, earthbound Western world rarely manage to match. Few of us, I think, live daily on the edge of eternity in the conscious way that the Puritans did, and we lose out as a result. For the extraordinary vivacity, even hilarity (yes, hilarity; you will find it in the sources), with which the Puritans lives stemmed, I believe, from the unflinching, matter-of-fact realism with which they prepared themselves for death, so as always to be found, as it were, packed up and ready to go. Reckoning with death brought appreciation of each day's

continued life, and the knowledge that God would eventually decide, without consulting them, when their work on earth was done brought energy for the work itself while they were still being given time to get on with it.[2]

We are ambassadors of Christ, and like any ambassador, we may at any moment be summoned home to give an account of what is going on at our post. Though looming judgment ought not terrify us, since we are saved by grace rather than works, it should change us. It should make us ask with each new morning, "Lord, knowing that *today* may be the last day of my life—perhaps even of the world—how shall I make things more suitable for your coming?" It should inspire us to continue in well-doing, even in the face of opposition, because, for all we know, the Lord of goodness may be on hand in five minutes.

Zeal for the coming Christ and love for people go together. Our practice of public goodness aims not to put people down but to win people to him before it is too late. What our culture needs these days is a vibrant, plausible, winsome Christianity. Intellectual and philosophical arguments are important and good, but they cannot stand alone. They must come from lives of people who have evidently been changed for the better by the God they profess. Do we love people enough, we must ask, to showcase—by how we talk, how we do business, how we do politics, and how we treat people—something of the goodness, justice, loyalty, beauty, and love of our true home? Why does Christ get such bad press in our day—or why does he often get no press at all? Could it be, at least in part, because we are not the winsome ambassadors we should be?

MAKING IT PERSONAL

1. Describe a situation in which the call to be Christ's ambassador weighed heavily on your conscience. What did you do about it?

2. Read over the following portion of the ancient *Letter to Diognetus:* "They [that is, Christians] dwell each in his native land, but only as resident aliens; they carry out all the tasks of a citizen, and endure all the burdens like foreigners; every foreign land is a native land to them, and every native land is a foreign land to them."

   Put into your own words the tension described here. Do you presently feel that tension? If so, why? If not, why not?

3. Read the book of Daniel or the book of Esther. How were the experiences of those people like our own? What lessons can be learned from Daniel and Esther about how to live as a "resident alien" today?

4. How does one live a life that is "squeaky clean" (above reproach at work, in one's financial dealings, and in one's relationships with the opposite sex) without being or appearing to be an unapproachable prude or a frightful bore?

5. How often do you think about your own mortality and that of the people you meet? What would it take for you to recover a sense of urgency about drawing others to Christ by living a life of positive goodness?

MARK 12:13-17

They sent some of the Pharisees and Herodians to Jesus to catch him in his words. They came to him and said, "Teacher, we know you are a man of integrity. You aren't swayed by men, because you pay no attention to who they are; but you teach the way of God in accordance with the truth. Is it right to pay taxes to Caesar or not? Should we pay or shouldn't we?"

But Jesus knew their hypocrisy. "Why are you trying to trap me?" he asked. "Bring me a denarius and let me look at it." They brought the coin, and he asked them, "Whose portrait is this? And whose inscription?"

"Caesar's," they replied.

Then Jesus said to them, "Give to Caesar what is Caesar's and to God what is God's."

And they were amazed at him.

Chapter Four

Two Kingdoms

A NUMBER OF YEARS AGO, WE STRIPPED THE SANCTUARY OF OUR church so that we could install a new carpet. One item we removed for the renovation was the American flag that for years had occupied a prominent place on the platform just behind the pulpit. When it came time to put everything back, my associate and I decided not to restore the flag to its customary spot but to set it up in the back of the church. We reasoned that, since Christ is Lord of all the nations and not simply of the United States, it did not make sense to make the symbol of our country quite so prominent in the place where we routinely gather to exalt him. We felt the force of this argument rather strongly since our worship service routinely drew large numbers of international students from the nearby university. We reasoned further that, since America ought to join the nations in submitting to Christ, the flag that symbolizes our land should "sit in the pews" with the rest of the congregation. Its traditional location next to the pulpit suggested too strong a link between what America says and what God says. It ran contrary to the humble sentiment expressed in the second stanza of "America the Beautiful":

America, America! God mend thine ev'ry flaw,
  Confirm thy soul in self-control, Thy liberty in law.

Despite our careful reasoning, our many reassurances that we loved our country, and our plan to leave the flag in the sanctuary (simply in another location), our decision drew a tremendous amount of heat from some people.

I will leave you to guess what we eventually did with the flag. For the moment let me try to answer, "Why all the heat?" The answer is that we do not always find it easy to "give to Caesar what is Caesar's and to God what is God's" (Mark 12:17). By those revolutionary words, Jesus taught us to distinguish a dual citizenship, but he did not make clear precisely how to do it. Christians can disagree strongly on what our double allegiance looks like in practice.

If you had been eligible, would you have fought in World War II? In Vietnam? In Desert Storm? Would you have flown bombing runs over Yugoslavia during NATO's air war with that nation? Chances are, your answers to these questions are not uniform. Sorting out our dual allegiance to God and to Uncle Sam is not simple.

If Christ is Lord of all, what right does Uncle Sam have to require any allegiance of me? Is it really possible to be both a sold-out Christian and a loyal American? And if some allegiance is due to my country, what are its limits? When (if ever) and how should I disobey the law or a representative of the government? How do I talk with fellow believers about "hot issues" without dividing or diverting the church? These are some of the questions we will try to address in the pages ahead.

Jesus Talks Politics

We should first take a closer look at Jesus' words in Mark 12:17. In their setting they are quite remarkable. A brilliant parry of his enemies' efforts to trap him, they also offer profound and revolutionary insight into the believer's relationship to government.

Before considering the words themselves, we should note simply that Jesus talked openly about tough political issues. Paying taxes to Caesar infuriated some people. The Jews of that time lived in Palestine under a foreign government, parallel in some ways to the French in Paris during the German occupation. Though cryptic and influenced by the ulterior motives of his opponents, Jesus' comments nevertheless took seriously the practical social problem presented by the question.

Jesus' readiness to talk politics reminds us of his claim to rule the whole of life. He means to reign not merely over my private world—the world of family, close friends, personal devotions, and so on—but my whole world, including my political life. Notice that Jesus answers the political question with a command, not just a suggestion: "Give to Caesar what is Caesar's and to God what is God's." Our Lord requires appropriate allegiances of us. He does not permit us to treat political questions as nonquestions, matters that we can take or leave because they are irrelevant to our obligation to him.

Two Kingdoms

According to Jesus, our obligation begins with the necessity of making a mental distinction between God's government and human government (we cannot render to each its due until we have done this). We make this distinction readily in our day, at least in theory. Beneficiaries of the remarkable political philosophy summarized by the First Amendment, we tend to scorn the Crusades, Oliver Cromwell's protectorate, and some modern Islamic states, all of which sought or seek to advance religion by force. I remember laughing grimly when I first heard of the "christianized" Roman army's practice of marching conquered people in chains through a river and pronouncing them baptized Christians (thereby subject to the emperor) as a result. Such behavior fails to distinguish between the two allegiances as our Lord does here—it equates a political undertaking with a religious one.

What is perhaps obvious to us was quite radical in Jesus' day, certainly for a Jew. Israel under Moses, Joshua, David, and the kings that followed him had been theocratic. God's doings in the world had found unique and particular expression in the undertakings of their nation. They dispossessed (in some cases, wiped out) people who did not share their beliefs, often at God's command. Though pious Jews knew that Yahweh was not just another local deity confined to Jerusalem,[1] they nevertheless believed that the Lord of heaven and earth had set his name in that city. When David went off to war, so did Yahweh.

The Jews of Jesus' day knew well the stories of Egypt's defeat, of the conquest of Canaan, of Gideon's and Samson's triumphs over the Midianites and the Philistines, and of David's and Solomon's expansive reigns. Many had drawn inspiration from the Lord's triumph in the desperate siege of Jerusalem during Jehoshaphat's reign: "Do not be afraid or discouraged because of this vast army. For the battle is not yours, but God's" (2 Chronicles 20:15). Many longed for a revived theocracy, savoring the memory of the Maccabean revolt against foreign apostasy and oppression. For many, Caesar was another Antiochus Epiphanes,[2] Rome was the kingdom of darkness, and Jesus was the new liberator. They anticipated political Israel in ascendancy with Jesus the son of David on the throne.

And then Jesus astounded them[3] by saying they should pay Caesar his due. Jesus implied here that the Jews actually owed Caesar something—a shocking statement under the circumstances.

A Radically New Pattern

There is much more than shock value in these words. Jesus ushered in a whole new understanding of the believer's political life. In distinguishing between the two governments, he effectively called us to stop thinking theocratically. We must no longer build or envision an earthly society as the location of God's exclusive interest and blessing. We must heed what Jesus said to Pilate, "My kingdom is not of this world" (John 18:36).

Our Lord's wise words, furthermore, provide us with a marvelous balance as we seek to relate to our government. On the one hand, he taught that we may in fact be both a sold-out Christian *and* a good American. Not to give our country its due is in fact to disobey Jesus, who commanded us to do that very thing. On the other hand, Jesus also taught that our ultimate allegiance cannot go to the United States, since that would be to deprive God of his due. In the words of one commentator, "Those words . . . gave to the civil power, under the protection of conscience, a sacredness it had never enjoyed and bounds it had never acknowledged, and they were the repudiation of absolutism and the inauguration of freedom."[4]

Sorting Out the Double Allegiance
How do we sort out our dual citizenship? Acknowledging both "Caesar" and God does not determine for us precisely what we owe to each.

Let's return to the problem of the flag in the sanctuary. Why did some people respond with so much emotion to our decision to move it? I know that at least part of the reaction grew from personal history. Every complainer had served honorably, or had been married to someone who had served honorably, in the armed forces. Some had seen combat in World War II. Moving the flag suggested to them that we cared little for the great freedoms we enjoy as Americans and the great cost at which those freedoms have been secured. My associate and I quickly realized that, whatever we did, we needed to respect the sacrifice and patriotism of many in our congregation.

The issues raised by the flag episode, however, go beyond personal feelings. Biblical scholars have long debated what Scripture teaches about the practical relationship between the two kingdoms. Some (called "positivists") argue that, since God ordains every government, submitting to my government is submitting to God. They justify their view by appealing to Romans 13:1-2: "Everyone must submit himself to the governing authorities, for there is no authority except that which God has established. The authorities that exist have been established by God. Consequently, he who rebels against the authority is rebelling against what God has instituted, and those who do so will bring judgment upon themselves." We honor God by honoring our country, since he sovereignly raised it up. Martin Luther championed this view when he strongly opposed the "murderous hordes of peasants"[5] who revolted against their overlords in the Peasants' Revolts of 1524 and 1525. American flags next to the pulpit in American churches might make sense, given this understanding—as might serving in the armed forces regardless of the conflict in view.

Positivists run into some practical difficulties when facing political injustice. They cannot, for example, easily justify the revolution that brought the United States into existence. Our Declaration of Independence argues that there are times "in the course of human events [when] it becomes necessary" to take up arms against a tyrannical government. On what grounds, it might be argued, is it *ever* necessary (or justifiable) to resist a government that God has sovereignly established? Even if it could be proven that British colonial rule in the 1770s was more oppressive than that of imperial Rome in Paul's day, the simple fact remains that, according to Romans 13, God set King George on the throne. To buck George, it would seem, is to buck God—a course of action difficult to justify. Positivists, in short, say, "Do nothing," when our hearts say, "Do something!"

As it turns out, our intuitive and practical critique of the positivist approach has strong theological grounds. We claim to believe in a God who is good and just. How, it is argued, can we claim to be his followers if we refuse to take up arms against the Hitlers of this world? Those who hold this view (often called "normativists") also appeal to Romans 13:3, where we read,

"Rulers hold no terror for those who do right, but for those who do wrong." They argue that such words describe a government as it *should be* according to God's design. When the government fails to live up to its God-given responsibility, then it may legitimately be resisted from within (by revolution) and from without (by war). Augustine, among others, speaks of "just war" from this perspective:

> Peace is the aim of wars. . . . Now when the victory goes to those who were fighting for the juster cause, can anyone doubt that the victory is a matter for rejoicing and the resulting peace is something to be desired? These things are good and undoubtedly they are gifts of God. But if the higher goods are neglected, which belong to the City on high, where victory will be serene in the enjoyment of eternal and perfect peace — if these goods are neglected and those other goods are so desired as to be the only goods, or are loved more than the goods which are believed to be higher, the inevitable consequence is fresh misery, and an increase of the wretchedness already there.[6]

Though the peace achieved when justice triumphs must never divert our hope from the peace that Christ alone will bring the nations (the point Augustine makes at the end of the above statement), the lesser peace is nonetheless cause for legitimate rejoicing. For this reason, bearing arms to secure that lesser peace is justifiable, a necessary evil in a world that is not yet fully redeemed. The propriety of displaying an American flag next to the pulpit might, given this approach, vary depending upon America's social policies at the time.

A difficulty with the normative view is that it does not precisely define when "Caesar" steps out of bounds, thus opening the door to violent attacks on government from any "liberator" who decides for whatever reason to appoint himself or herself to the task.

There remains at least one other approach. John Yoder, a modern promoter of this view, calls us to "revolutionary subordination"[7] on the basis of the teaching and example of Christ. In Yoder's understanding, America (like every government) exists with God's permission, and we must therefore respect it. But our country's days are numbered, since at the cross Jesus demonstrated and instituted a radically new system of governance, based not upon power but upon love. We submit to our government, but we do so in love, not fear, knowing that it is only a matter of time before that old order will disappear. Thus we are free, even as we submit, for our hearts and hopes are not tied to human government at all. Yoder says, "The subordinate person becomes a free ethical agent when he voluntarily accedes to his subordination in the power of Christ instead of bowing to it either fatalistically or resentfully."[8]

Those who hold this third view (often called "pacifists") permit political resistance, even encourage it in the face of oppression. But that resistance must be nonviolent, since to resist violently compromises Christ's ethic. For the same reason, pacifists refuse to bear arms. Menno Simons, a sixteenth-century priest after whom the Mennonites take their name, wrote: "The regenerated do not go to war, nor engage in strife. They are the children of peace who have beaten their swords into plowshares and their spears into pruning hooks, and know of no war. . . . Since we are to be conformed to the image of Christ, how can we then fight our enemies with the sword? . . . Spears and swords of iron we leave to those who, alas, consider human blood and swine's blood of well-nigh equal value."[9] American pacifists might well be reluctant to display an American flag next to the pulpit, since that too readily equates a human government with Christ's radically different administration. And, of course, they would not bear arms.

In my view the "normative" position makes the best sense of both Scripture and life. According to the New Testament, we live in the "last days," the season in the history of redemption bordered by the first and second comings of Christ. This means that we are caught in the tension between what theologians call the "already" and the "not yet." On the one hand, Christ has died, has risen, and is now ruling at the right hand of God. He has triumphed over the kingdoms of this world, both seen and unseen, and it is only a matter of time before his ethic of love and goodness will define every part of human social life, both private and public. On the other hand, we await Christ's return. Until that day, and even on that day, he will restrain and punish human cruelty and oppression, by force if necessary.

Living with Two Ethics

Living as we do between Christ's two advents, we must find a way to live with both ethics at once—with both the Sermon on the Mount and with Romans 13. We do so by distinguishing between our behavior as individuals and our behavior as agents of our government.

Two scenes from the film *Saving Private Ryan* illustrate the distinction.[10] The first occurs on D-Day at the moment when the American soldiers finally gain mastery of a bunker from which German soldiers have been slaughtering their fellows all day. The Germans emerge, hands in the air signifying their surrender, and they are shot dead at point-blank range. Up until the point of the German surrender, the American soldiers were shooting to kill, or at least to put the German defenders out of action. In so doing, they were serving as agents of the state in an international "police action" whose purpose was to bring to an end an evil regime. They were, in short, legitimately using force as a kind of necessary evil to overthrow a greater evil. At the moment of the German surrender, however, a second ethic should have kicked in. A Christian soldier covering the surrendering Germans might well have been tempted to revenge the death of his comrades, but for Christ's sake he should have resisted that temptation and sought to protect and meet the needs of the POWs.

In the second scene an American platoon encounters a German machine-gun nest in a field. They storm the nest and capture it, leaving all but one German soldier dead. In the process their medic (a noncombatant) is killed by the surviving German. Angry at their commander for having ordered the attack in the first place (they could have simply gone around the field), and murderous toward the captured German who has just killed their friend, the Americans make their captive dig his own grave, fully intending to kill him. The mutinous standoff that ensues between the officer (who will not allow the killing) and his men nearly issues in more bloodshed. In this case the behavior of the commander vividly illustrates the dual ethic we have been considering. First, he orders the attack on the German machine gunners, an order that legitimately involves killing. But then, after the surrender, he refuses to allow himself or his men to give in to personal vengeance. He acts, in other words, by the ethics of the kingdom to come.

It must be extremely difficult to live by these two standards, especially in a battle situation. It must at times appear absurd. But that does not make it wrong to try. A Christian police officer may legitimately use his gun to keep a violent teenager from shooting his partner. But once he subdues the teenager, he may not in good conscience harm the teen, even if the teen has killed his partner in the process of being subdued. The difficulty and seeming absurdity in situations like this may distress us,[11] but they should not surprise us. Our world is still fallen. Christ has come: He is working through us to make things better, but we must await his return before all is made right.

A Love Too Broad to Settle in One Place

Our Lord's distinction between the two kingdoms does more than point us in a helpful direction as we try to make sense of our allegiance to our government. It also fans our hopes by pointing toward his great redemptive plan for the nations of the world. Remember that in differentiating between Caesar and God, Jesus was disassembling the theocracy. No longer was God going to associate his reign with one particular people. And this is so, not because God no longer has a saving interest in any nation, but because he has a saving interest in every nation. Jesus knew that with his coming God was ushering in a whole new scenario for the world. Israel was to lose its "monopoly" on God, not because God did not love Israel, but because he chose not to love Israel *only*. The kingdom Jesus announced in his preaching and inaugurated on Pentecost counts as its citizens people living all around the world.

Billy Graham came to Long Island for a crusade in the 1990s. The internationality of the New York metropolitan region found vivid expression in those who gathered. I remember with delight a huge Korean choir singing "Amazing Grace" in their native tongue, Steve Green singing a gospel tune in Spanish, and a Chinese friend doing spontaneous translation for a large delegation of Mandarin speakers. Most moving of all were the deaf signers, who with exquisite grace of movement brought all that was said and sung into the silent world of the deaf who had come to "hear." Observing all this, I thought with great joy, *Now* this *is the kingdom of God, the reign of the King of kings breaking in upon every tribe and nation!*

Surely God has blessed America and continues to do so. Surely many Christians and much Christian thinking have influenced us for the good down through the years. But to confuse these facts with the notion that we are in some special sense God's country is to forget the distinction Jesus drew and to shrink God's gracious plans. God's love is simply too great to be bottled up in one language or in one location or in one people.

Reining In Our Political Expectations

Distinguishing between the two kingdoms helps keep us politically realistic and sane. For if we give God his due, then no human governor or government will be worthy of either our highest hopes or our unthinking allegiance. We all suffer in some way from the utopian impulse, the idolatrous voice that urges us to lean on people to accomplish more than they are capable of. Sometimes the impulse proves ironic, even silly, as when our euphoria over the election of our favorite candidate turns to bitterness in six months—both reactions driven by unrealistic expectations.

At other times abandonment to the utopian impulse yields unspeakable misery, as the twentieth century amply illustrated. The Russian people and later the German people gave way to the impulse in allowing the political promises of Marxism and fascism to obscure their vision, thus unleashing a spate of horrific "experiments" in social engineering worldwide.

Christian citizens know that God will not share his glory with another (see Isaiah 42:8) and that the key to social transformation must therefore lie outside of human effort. We realize that simply spending more money or implementing new programs will not solve the problems of drugs in the city, violence in the home, and chaos in the classroom. Our realism makes us patient with the imperfections of government and its agents (the president, the mayor, the police), knowing that the power for deep societal change does not come from that quarter. We criticize less and pray more, not as an alternative to working as best we can for a better society, but as an expression of our reliance, as we work, on the Ruler of all.

Today's cynic is yesterday's idealist. Christian citizens do not give way to political cynicism—or to the apathy that often accompanies it—because from the start we have been realists. We carry on the best we can to make a fallen world better, but we never forget that we await the kingdom of God, a kingdom that Christ taught us never to equate with something we can produce. Caesar and God are not the same.

MAKING IT PERSONAL

1. Consider the American flag story at the opening of the chapter. Where would you have placed the flag and why?

2. Read Lord Acton's interpretation of Jesus' famous statement "Give to Caesar what is Caesar's and to God what is God's": "Those words . . . gave to the civil power, under the protection of conscience, a sacredness it had never enjoyed and bounds it had never acknowledged, and they were the repudiation of absolutism and the inauguration of freedom."

   Use your own language to describe the balance that Acton believes Jesus' words bring to the way we should order our political life. Give modern illustrations of the "protection of conscience" and of the absence of such protection. How, practically, do we treat the role of a police officer (or of a senator) as sacred while at the same time putting boundaries around that role?

3. Compare (using the "positivist," "normativist," and "pacifist" distinctions found in this chapter) how you would have behaved toward Hitler if you were a German citizen in 1939 with how you would have behaved toward King George if you were an American colonist in 1776. Why the difference, if any?

4. Read Matthew 5–7 (the Sermon on the Mount) and Romans 13:1-7 (where Paul speaks of submitting to the government). How, taken together, do these texts help us sort out our double allegiance to both God and our government? (The illustrations from *Saving Private Ryan* found in this chapter may be of help.)

5. The end of the theocracy means that God does not give special status to any particular nation or culture. This means, among other things, that we must temper our nationalism with a genuine love for and interest in all peoples. Inventory your relationships with internationals. Do you have any friends from other nations and cultures? If not, what might you do to cultivate some? Do you need to repent of racial prejudice? Do you look down upon certain races or nations? Do you often make snap judgments about people

solely on the basis of their skin color or nationality? During Desert Storm, did you think of Iraqis as inferior, and did you take secret pleasure in the effectiveness of our "smart bomb" campaign?

ROMANS 13:1-7

Everyone must submit himself to the governing authorities, for there is no authority except that which God has established. The authorities that exist have been established by God. Consequently, he who rebels against the authority is rebelling against what God has instituted, and those who do so will bring judgment on themselves. For rulers hold no terror for those who do right, but for those who do wrong. Do you want to be free from fear of the one in authority? Then do what is right and he will commend you. For he is God's servant to do you good. But if you do wrong, be afraid, for he does not bear the sword for nothing. He is God's servant, an agent of wrath to bring punishment on the wrongdoer. Therefore, it is necessary to submit to the authorities, not only because of possible punishment but also because of conscience.

This is why you pay taxes, for the authorities are God's servants, who give their full time to governing. Give everyone what you owe him: If you owe taxes, pay taxes; if revenue, then revenue; if respect, then respect; if honor, then honor.

1 PETER 2:13,17

Submit yourselves for the Lord's sake to every authority instituted among men. . . . Show proper respect to everyone: Love the brotherhood of believers, fear God, honor the king.

Chapter Five

GIVING CAESAR
HIS DUE

SPEAKING AT GETTYSBURG IN NOVEMBER OF 1863, ABRAHAM Lincoln urged his listeners to dedicate themselves "to the great task remaining before us—that from these honored dead we take increased devotion to that cause for which they gave the last full measure of devotion." By "last full measure of devotion," he meant the sacrifice of their lives, a sacrifice made for high purposes: "that [their] nation might live," and that "this nation, under God, shall have a new birth of freedom—and that government of the people, by the people, and for the people shall not perish from the earth."

Lincoln evidently believed that preserving the union and ending slavery in that union were causes worth dying for. Robert E. Lee, a man whose faith in Christ was perhaps deeper even than Lincoln's, felt that the preservation of Virginia's freedom from northern intrusion was also a cause worth dying for. Their aims certainly clashed, but these two great leaders agreed that serving God and serving one's country, even to the point of death, may be compatible. They agreed, in other words, with Augustine's notion of just war.

Though I may never be asked to die for my country, giving "Caesar" his due may legitimately call me to many other sacrifices, some of which we will consider in this chapter.

Separate Worlds?

First, we need to look again at Jesus' command in its first-century context, together with Paul's and Peter's elaborations of it. Jesus' endorsement of Caesar must certainly have shocked many of his fellow Jews. Caesar was a foreign oppressor. Somewhat wiser in his tolerance of Judaism than Antiochus Epiphanes,[1] he nevertheless ruled as a pagan Gentile in the land that God had given to Abraham. To make matters worse, he counted himself divine. "Tiberius Caesar Augustus, Son of the Divine Augustus" appeared on the coin that Jesus asked to be brought to him when confronted with the question about paying taxes (Mark 12:13-17).

We are rightly astounded that Jesus should have tolerated such an inscription, not to mention acquiescing in its author's demand for money. And yet Jesus did. Why? Did our Lord believe that God rules one area of life (the religious and spiritual one) while human beings rule another (the political and social one)? Did Jesus, in other words, see life as made up of at least two nonintersecting spheres—what we might call the kingdom of God and the kingdoms of humankind—in which different rules of conduct apply? Can the Christian be one sort of person in church and another sort of person in government and public life? This cannot be what Jesus meant.

Perhaps Jesus was teaching that the different spheres belong to different types of people. "Pagans" and worldly types, in this understanding, go into the lower world of politics, while the more spiritual types do evangelism, church work, and missions. Given the prevailing cynicism about politics, Christians might well be tempted to think in such terms. But they would be wrong.

Jesus commanded us to give Caesar his due, not because he saw Caesar's world as somehow independent from God's, but for the opposite reason. Jesus knew that his Father reigned as absolute sovereign over every sphere of life, including the political one. God and God alone brings men and women and governments (even Rome) into power, and they are to be treated with respect for this very reason. As Paul put it, "Everyone must submit himself to the governing authorities, for there is no authority except that which God has established" (Romans 13:1).

One Supreme Authority: The Bible's
Consistent Message

Neither Jesus nor Paul initiated this notion. Even during the days of the theocracy, God repeatedly taught and demonstrated his universal reign: "Look at the nations and watch—and be utterly amazed. For I am going to do something in your days that you would not believe, even if you were told. I am raising up the Babylonians, that ruthless and impetuous people, who sweep across the whole earth to seize dwelling places not their own" (Habakkuk 1:5). The nation to which Habakkuk referred here was the sixth century B.C. equivalent of Nazi Germany. He described the Babylonians as "ruthless," as a "law to themselves," with "horses . . . swifter than leopards" (remember the blitzkrieg?), as "guilty men, whose own strength is their god" (verses 6-8,11). What shocked and troubled the prophet most deeply was neither the impending judgment on Israel nor the ruthless evil of the Babylonians. His grief arose from God's assertion that *he* would raise up this people, for Habakkuk rightly contended, "My God, my Holy One, . . . your eyes are too pure to look on evil; you cannot tolerate wrong" (verses 12-13). While admitting the mystery here, and acknowledging that God is not to be blamed for the evil that people do to each other, we must also agree that no nation—not even an evil one—arises apart from his holy and wise administration.

Nebuchadnezzar, who reigned in Babylon from 605 to 562 B.C., fulfilled the prophecy of Habakkuk. Rising to power after his rout of the Egyptians at Carchemish in 605, he conquered all of Syria and Palestine, including Judah and Jerusalem, which fell to him in 597 after a brutal siege. Of those few who survived the carnage and famine, nearly all were transported to Babylon. For all his arrogant self-assurance, this rapacious monarch came so powerfully under the influence of his godly captives and their Lord that he learned to praise him. The Lord made him mad for a season, and upon his return to sanity, he wrote:

> "I praised the Most High; I honored and glorified him
>   who lives forever.
> His dominion is an eternal dominion;
>   his kingdom endures from generation to generation.
> All the peoples of the earth
>   are regarded as nothing.
> He does as he pleases
>   with the powers of heaven
>   and the peoples of the earth. (Daniel 4:34-35)

God made clear his reign not only during but also at the end of the exile. Around 750 B.C.—long before the rise of the Babylonian Empire—Isaiah foretold the name of the Persian king who would overthrow the Babylonians in 539 B.C. and issue a decree permitting Jews to return to Judah:

> This is what the LORD says to his anointed,
>   to Cyrus, whose right hand I take hold of
>   to subdue nations before him
>   and to strip kings of their armor. . . .
> For the sake of Jacob my servant,
>   of Israel my chosen,
> I summon you by name
>   and bestow on you a title of honor,
>   though you do not acknowledge me.
> I am the LORD, and there is no other. (Isaiah 45:1,4-5)[2]

Rulers do not have to know the Lord—or even exist yet—for God to reign over and through them. The great prophet Jeremiah, who lived through much political change and personal misery at the hands of wicked people, summarized well what we have been saying. Pronouncing for the Lord, he said, "With my great power and outstretched arm I made the earth and its people and the animals that are on it, and I give it to anyone I please" (Jeremiah 27:5).

Why the rise of America? Why the collapse of the Soviet Union? Why did the American Revolution produce a democracy and the French Revolution produce a dictator? How did the British Isles escape the violent upheaval that the eighteenth century brought to France? Why the triumph of Milosevic's butcheries in Kosovo, and of Gandhi's pacifism in India? How do we explain the political and economic tranquillity of Costa Rica when all around that nation Latin America has endured chaos? How do we explain the peaceful end to apartheid in South Africa, contrary to all expectation? Why did the twentieth century see the rise of so many genocidal regimes? The secondary (and not insignificant) reasons are numerous and invite careful analysis, but the deepest cause for all these realities is the Lord himself. For a host of purposes, many of which we cannot fully understand, God establishes the nations and their rulers. Jesus knew this and taught us for this reason to give them their due.

Eyes to See the Deeper Reality

While we must never submit blindly to any authority (we will discuss civil disobedience later), we should nevertheless give more than grudging support to those whom the Lord has placed over us. Paul counseled slaves this way: "Slaves, obey your earthly masters in everything; and do it, not only when their eye is on you and to win their favor, but with sincerity of heart and reverence for the Lord. Whatever you do, work at it with all your heart, as working for the Lord, not for men. . . . It is the Lord Christ you are serving" (Colossians 3:22-24).[3] Paul urged upon slaves the faith to see the Lord's hand behind that of the master, and to draw their hopes for justice and their motivation for service not from the master they could see but from the one they could not see. Though modern public authority differs dramatically from ancient slave ownership and imperial oversight, the same principle applies to us today. The believer sees God's hand behind the process and respects the authority from the heart, for God's sake.

On one occasion my pastoral duties obliged me to give testimony at a hearing that led to the enforced hospitalization of one of my parishioners. The hearing took place in a small hospital room adjacent to the place where my friend lay strapped to a gurney for his own protection. In addition to me, the assembly consisted of a clerk, two attorneys (one representing the interests of the community and the other the interests of my friend), and an elderly, wheelchair-bound judge. We chatted in a friendly, if subdued, fashion until the clerk called us to order. At that point a remarkable seriousness, a kind of holiness, settled upon us. I will never forget the sense of accountability that we all (including the judge) seemed to feel as we considered the fate of my friend. Though no one mentioned God's name, except in the oath taking, his presence as the "judge behind the judge" was palpable in the deference given to his human counterpart and in the care and sensitivity with which that counterpart heard the evidence and rendered his decision.

As I drove home afterward, I could not help reflecting on the biblical underpinnings of what I had just experienced. I thanked God for the measure to which those underpinnings still exercise their influence in our country, despite the increasing secularization of our time. Knowing how my friend might have been treated in another time or in a different culture increased my resolve to honor the people who are part of the governmental process in America.

Beyond the Merely Legal

Why should I pay taxes? Why should I treat with respect the

officer who has just given me a $75 speeding ticket? Why do I treat with respect the officer who has just rudely cited me for something I did not do (I will never forget this happening to me as a teenager)? Why do I obey the law? Why, like Esther, Daniel, Paul, and (to cite a modern example) Dietrich Bonhoeffer, do I speak with respect to my captors?[4] Why do I fight willingly in the armed forces when called, unless for reasons of conscience I feel I cannot? And why, if I am a conscientious objector, am I humbly prepared to take the consequences for my stand?

Do I act this way simply because I might get into trouble if I do not? Is my civic behavior, in other words, limited only by the question "Can I get away with it?" Should we respect government and its agents only when we agree with them? Should we honor them only because they do not at the moment interfere with our private rights and pleasures? Not if we are faithful to Scripture. We respect "Caesar" because we respect God; when we dishonor "Caesar," we dishonor God.

Too many Americans, including Christian Americans, seem content these days with satisfying the letter of the civil law. The phenomenal rise in litigation owes itself in large part to our willingness to be content with asking, "Is it legal?" and "Is it acceptable?" We should also be asking, "Is it moral?" and "Is it good for the community in which God has placed me?" Because we live under Christ, we should have a conscience attuned to whether a course of action is right before God, not simply tolerable before people. And our conscience should apply itself across the board, in every part of life: environmental concerns, energy, hiring and firing, wage setting, social welfare, awards in liability cases, and so on.

Is it right, I must ask, to sue my town for $10 million simply because I know I can win? Should a Christian builder feel free to build in an environmentally sensitive place once he has ascertained that the law will not be able to stop him? Should Christians search high and low for tax loopholes? Should a Christian CEO order the buyout of a small business without considering the hardship the people of that company and its customers might experience, simply because she knows she may legally do so? Should a Christian teenager accelerate madly down a neighborhood street full of children, satisfied simply because he remains under the speed limit? Should a Christian play the state lottery simply because it is legal, or should she shop all day Sunday just because the mall is open for business? Is it okay to watch an R-rated movie or drink myself into oblivion just because I have reached the age at which such behavior is now legal? Should a Christian researcher experiment on aborted fetal tissue, or should a believer pregnant from in vitro fertilization discard the unused embryos simply because the law does not forbid such behavior?

I ask these questions gently, knowing that the proper answers are not in every case obvious. Nevertheless, I ask them, as we all should, since what is legal and possible is not necessarily right. We must all answer to Christ and not simply to the human magistrate.

No legal system can possibly cover every contingency. This means that when we abandon ourselves to the merely legal, we invite not the triumph of the good but the triumph of the skillful, or the equivalent in our day of "might makes right."[5] The legal practitioner who can work the system the best comes out on top.

Furthermore, abandoning ourselves to the merely legal threatens the community, both in the act itself and in its results. A community whose members ask only "Is it legal?" is like a family whose members ask only "Can I get away with this?" Neither will last very long. A community whose members ask only "Is it legal?" discovers that the only way to solve disputes is by suing, a process that may give some satisfaction but rarely improves relationships. How, we must ask, can a community of adversaries be a community?

Godliness Is the Key to Civic Health

Such tragic fallout should bolster our commitment, for deeper reasons, never to be content with the merely legal. We serve Christ, and for that reason we care always and most deeply about what is right. I know that the law cannot make me love my neighbor as I love myself, but I do so anyway because America's laws do not alone bind me.

The eighteenth-century French philosopher Jean-Jacques Rousseau wrote, "Far from winning the hearts of the citizens for the state, [the Christian faith] removes them from it, as from all earthly things. I know nothing that is more actively opposed to the social spirit."[6] We have been noting something quite different. Despite Rousseau's concern over divided loyalties, the Christian turns out in fact to be an excellent citizen. Statesman and orator Daniel Webster said, "Whatever makes men good Christians makes them good citizens." Reformation leader John Calvin wrote, "The obedience to leaders and magistrates is always linked to the worship and fear of God." We love our country, not because we worship it (no "good Christian" could do that), nor because it is always right (no "wise Christian" would ever admit that), but because we trust the divine wisdom of the sovereign one who has placed us where we are and commanded us to love our neighbor in that place. To use the apostle Paul's words, "It is necessary to submit to the authorities, not only because of possible punishment but also because of conscience" (Romans 13:5). Charles Colson summarizes well what we have been saying:

> Christians who are faithful to Scripture should be patriots in the best sense of that word. They are "the salvation of the commonwealth," said Augustine, for they fulfill the highest role of citizenship. Not because they are forced to or even choose to, not out of any chauvinistic motivations or allegiances to a political leader, but because they love and obey the King who is above all temporal leaders. . . . Since the state cannot legislate love, Christian citizens bring a humanizing element to civic life, helping to produce the spirit by which people do good out of compassion, not compulsion.[7]

An extraordinary revival, later called the Great Awakening, swept through the American colonies in the 1740s. What distinguished that revival from its often frothy and superficial counterpart in our day was its civic impact. Historian Benjamin Tremble wrote:

> There seemed to be a general conviction, that all the ways of man were before the eyes of the Lord. It was the opinion of men of discernment and sound judgment, who had the best opportunities of knowing the feelings and general state of the people for that period, that bags of gold and silver . . . might, with safety, have been laid in the streets, and that no man would have converted them to his own use. Theft, wantonness, intemperance, profaneness, Sabbath breaking, and other gross sins, seemed to be put away.[8]

Imagine what sort of a nation we might be today if in significant numbers we were to bring our public behavior under the scrutiny of a biblically educated conscience. Imagine, in other words, what it might be like if God were deeply feared by many Americans, not as a top-down government policy, but as a bottom-up grassroots reality. Though utopia would still elude us, things would improve, perhaps dramatically. As more people began policing themselves and the communities in which they are involved, crime would diminish, along with the cost of law enforcement and incarceration. Domestic violence, both physical and psychological, would begin to give way before the happy pressure of love and faithfulness, with incalculable benefits to children (and to their children after them). The demand for drugs would diminish as increasing numbers of people found meaning and love under the reign of Christ. Integrity in business would be more common, reducing the necessity for bureaucratic monitoring and litigation, both of which absorb colossal amounts of time, energy, and money. Hope and trust would exercise a stronger influence upon the tone of public discourse, occasioning more courtesy and less accusation, more creativity and less complaint, more optimism and less cynicism. Mercy, generosity, and justice, rising from the grassroots of the culture, would build the sort of quality community that a government could never successfully impose.

We are wrong and foolish to expect heaven on earth. We must await Christ's return for that. But we are equally wrong to deny the power of Christ to work significant change upon a culture whose people take him seriously enough to love, for his sake, the land and people where he has placed them.

MAKING IT PERSONAL

1. Winston Churchill made the following observation before the House of Commons on November 11, 1947: "It has been said that democracy is the worst form of government — except for all those other forms that have been tried from time to time."

   Discuss Churchill's remark in the light of Romans 13:1-7, a text that describes government as a "necessary evil" instituted by God to keep human beings from social self-destruction. Why, according to Romans 13, is human government necessary? To what "evils" do human governments contribute? Think not only of foreign governments but also of the United States: campaign financing, prison population demographics, taxation policies, police "profiling."

2. View the film *Dead Man Walking* and discuss capital punishment in light of the film and the following passages: Genesis 9:5-6, Matthew 5:38-45, and Romans 13:1-7. Some questions to consider:

   (a) Could the nun have been as effective in reaching the murderer if she had believed that capital punishment was morally justifiable?

   (b) Would the murderer have come to admit his crime if he did not know that he was going to die?

    (c) Does the film depict capital punishment as a "necessary evil"?

    (d) Does Scripture call the parents of the slain teenagers to respond to the murderer in the same way that it calls the government to respond to him?

    (e) What particulars about America's renewed practice of capital punishment need reform?

3. Pick two or three of the ethical questions listed on pages 65-66 and try to develop a thoughtful answer to them. As you discuss them, try to articulate

    (a) what circumstances might modify your answer,

    (b) what effect different attitudes of heart might have on your answer,

    (c) what further facts you would need to know before you could answer, and

    (d) what biblical principles and passages might apply to the issue.

4. Read aloud the following statement by Charles Colson:

    Christians who are faithful to Scripture should be patriots in the best sense of that word. They are "the salvation of the commonwealth," said Augustine, for they fulfill the highest role of citizenship. Not because they are forced to or even choose to, not out of any chauvinistic motivations or allegiances to a political leader, but because they love and obey the King who is above all temporal leaders. . . . Since the state cannot legislate love, Christian citizens bring a humanizing element to civic life, helping to produce the spirit by which people do good out of compassion, not compulsion.

    Share some examples of things you have done freely for the public good—not because the laws of America required it, and not because you were afraid of getting in trouble if you did not do it, but simply because you knew it was pleasing to God and helpful to your community.

MATTHEW 22:37-38

"Love the Lord your God with all your heart and with all your soul and with all your mind." This is the first and greatest commandment.

MATTHEW 10:34-39

Do not suppose that I have come to bring peace to the earth. I did not come to bring peace, but a sword. For I have come to turn

"a man against his father,
a daughter against her
    mother,
a daughter-in-law against her
    mother-in-law —
a man's enemies will be the
    members of his own
    household."

Anyone who loves his father or mother more than me is not worthy of me; anyone who loves his son or daughter more than me is not worthy of me; and anyone who does not take his cross and follow me is not worthy of me. Whoever finds his life will lose it, and whoever loses his life for my sake will find it.

Chapter Six

GIVING GOD HIS DUE

⁂

NEAR THE BEGINNING OF HIS NOVEL *THE SUM OF ALL FEARS*, TOM Clancy introduces us to Father Tim Riley, a savvy Jesuit who teaches at Georgetown. When asked about Father Tim's trustworthiness regarding a delicate matter of state, CIA deputy director Jack Ryan answers, "Father Tim is an American citizen, and he's not a security risk. But he's also a priest, and he has taken vows to what he naturally considers an authority higher than the Constitution. You can trust the man to honor all his obligations, but don't forget what all those obligations are."[1]

We must not forget what all our obligations are. We must love America for Christ's sake, not for its own sake, which means that we will love America deeply but neither blindly nor absolutely. Our deepest obligation will always be to Christ. Christ spoke of bringing a sword, not because his prime intention was to divide people from each other, but because he knew that the allegiance he demanded would inevitably lead to that division.

Consider again the dispute over paying taxes to Caesar. If the Roman denarius belonged to Caesar because it bore the impress of his image, to whom do you suppose we belong, given the image we bear by creation and, if Christian, by redemption?[2] Though Jesus did not make this point explicitly in that interchange, we can be sure from his treatment of people and his loyalty to Scripture that he believed it.[3] We belong absolutely to the King of kings, and our efforts to be good citizens express that deeper loyalty. For this reason, we respectfully refuse to obey "Caesar" when he commands of us something that Scripture forbids (we will discuss this more fully in chapter eight).

I had to grapple with this issue during my last year in college. The Vietnam War had escalated to the point where draft deferments were no longer available for those who, like me, were contemplating graduate school. What is worse, a national draft lottery had given me a low number, which all but guaranteed that I would be drafted upon graduation. What was I, as a follower of Jesus, to do? Certainly I did not want to risk losing my life, especially since I was engaged to be married at the time. But I knew that fear did not constitute a legitimate reason for denying my country its due. In addition, I was genuinely confused about the ethics of the conflict. I believed in the just war theory (we discussed this in chapter four) and found myself wondering about the fundamental justice of our nation's involvement in Vietnam. As it turned out, while still struggling with the ethics of it all, I flunked my army physical and received a permanent exemption. But for this eleventh-hour development, I may well have had to respectfully refuse to serve my country out of love for Jesus.

Refusing "Caesar" when we are morally and spiritually compelled to is only half of our responsibility. If I am to "give to God what is God's," especially in our democratic country, I will work to bring his standards to bear upon it. That is, I will love America and its people enough to promote those things that please my heavenly King and resist those things that displease him. I will be an active citizen, never assuming that something is right simply because I am comfortable with it or because it is American. In this sense, Rousseau's concern about the "divided loyalty" of Christian citizens noted in chapter five has a certain basis: "Jesus came in order to set up a spiritual kingdom on earth; thereby the theological system was separated from the political system, and this in turn meant that the state ceased to be *one* state, and that inherent tension emerged, which has never since ceased to agitate the Christian peoples."[4]

Legislating Morality

Working for social change can take many forms, as we shall see over the following chapters. Let us consider for the moment one possible way: legislation.

Is it right for a government to enact laws regulating the lives of active homosexuals in the military and in public school teaching? Should a community be permitted to take legal action to shut down its "adult" bookstores? Should believers seek to pass a sanctity-of-human-life amendment? There are those who argue vehemently that such actions abuse the sort of moral freedom that our Constitution was designed to protect. Justice and the principles of civil rights, they argue, demand that morality not be legislated. Christians, they complain, have no right to impose their ethics upon our pluralistic country. Such imposition breaches the dividing wall that properly stands between church and state.

The issue of legislating morality, or (to make the matter specifically Christian) of seeking to change for Christ's sake the laws of America, is complex. If we say no to the question of whether we should try to legislate morality, we must then ask whether the lordship of Christ really means anything to us. But if we say yes, we must immediately confront other questions, like "Which morals do we seek to legislate, and why?" If we promote laws regulating homosexual behavior, should we not with even more fervor promote Sabbath observance laws? After all, worshiping God is the first, and most important, of his commandments. And if some among us seek to regulate homosexual behavior, which behavior should be addressed and why — private sex acts, public sex acts, gay marriage, teaching in the public schools, serving in the armed forces? And if such laws are enacted, how should those who break them be punished?

Deriving civil laws from Scripture and applying them in modern America demands careful thought beyond the scope of our efforts here. We will have to be content with an observation and three distinctions that should help us navigate the difficult waters.

Everyone Legislates Morality

Those who argue that the law must never promote ethical values are not thinking very clearly. After all, what are the laws of our nation if they are not the legal expression of the values we hold? By prohibiting theft, drunk driving, embezzlement, and child abuse, and by writing standards for commerce, affirmative action, environmental protection, and divorce proceedings, we codify the values we believe in. Those who cry, "You must not legislate morality!" are themselves advocating a certain set of values (a morality, if you will) and bringing it to bear upon the process of lawmaking.

We simply cannot escape the influence of values. They may be good values or bad values—depending upon our perspective—but they will always be the basis upon which we do our lawmaking. When, therefore, someone cries, "How dare you legislate morality!" what he or she really means is "How dare you legislate *that* particular morality, since I disagree with it." The proper question is not *whether* ethics should be enforced but rather *which* ethics should be enforced. If Christ's people do not stand up legislatively for the values that please their heavenly King, then someone else may stand up for values that displease him.

Distinguishing Between Theocracy and Influence

Advancing Christ's standards through legislation calls for wisdom. It demands first that we lean against the tendency to try to make America Christian by force of law. We must distinguish, in other words, between the Christian takeover of government and the Christian influence upon government.

Some of us are nostalgic about what we perceive to have been a Christian Golden Age, and this dream fires us with zeal to recapture that past. While it is true that for many years Christianity enjoyed a privileged position in American public life (often to the benefit of that life), those times were not without their problems. The community that had fled England in search of religious freedom drove Roger Williams from its borders because he championed freedom of conscience and justice for the Indians. Thomas Jefferson (one of many deists among the Founding Fathers) excised large portions of his Bible to conform it to his less than orthodox faith. And slavery was both tolerated and defended until after the mid-nineteenth century.

The present, even more than the past, should check our zeal to force Christianity upon our land. The American population today is far more diverse, both ethnically and religiously, than it once was. The concern in the eighteenth century was that no particular brand of Christianity should gain political ascendancy; today America welcomes a seemingly endless variety of faiths—religious and nonreligious. Any approach taken by Christians to promote the values of Christ in public life must deal with this reality. If we seek to circumvent pluralism in the name of Christ, or to blast a path through it, we will in the end produce a culture that tolerates a Christian presence even less than it does now.

The most important reason not to make America legally Christian is that God forbids us to. We noted earlier that theocracy belongs to an earlier stage in redemptive history. Edmund Clowney warns:

> No state, no freedom fighter today can lay claim to Israel's theocratic calling as warriors of God's covenant. The new Israel is the church of Jesus Christ, and he has forbidden the sword to the church. Under the lordship of Christ, the Kingdom of God does take form in the church, but through mightier weapons than the sword: weapons, as Paul affirms, that can reduce every towering imagination of the rebellious human heart. No other weapons can advance Christ's

Kingdom. The political renovation of the world awaits his return, for he is the sole monarch of the universe.[5]

We must diligently distinguish in thought and practice between trying to make America God's nation (which is wrong) and seeking to use lawful means in a sensitive way to promote values that please Christ (which is right). A pithy summary of Christian influence upon American culture appeared in PBS president Ervin Duggan's remarks at the Davidson College 1994 fall convocation:

> Only years after leaving this place did I realize that the religious tradition honored by those starchy old Calvinists [Davidson's founders] was what brought into being many of the things I cherished most. The teaching that all persons are created in the image of God, for example: that religious idea gives the only transcendent depth and meaning to our notions of human rights, of human beings as sacred. The ancient doctrine of Original Sin, for example: it led James Madison and John Adams to insist upon limitations of power, upon a system of checks and balances. The Judeo-Christian idea of covenantal laws and relationships, for example: this led, in time, to modern democratic constitutions and the Bill of Rights. Indeed, our modern ideas of tolerance and pluralism owe much to great assertions of human universality like that of the apostle Paul: "I am persuaded that in Christ, there is neither Jew nor Greek."[6]

Though we may find this distinction difficult to make in the nitty-gritty, and though we may find ourselves disagreeing with each other in the effort, we nevertheless must humbly try.

Distinguishing Between Private and Corporate Callings

I remember leaving my church in Virginia early one Sunday afternoon and discovering that during the service a well-intentioned church member had placed leaflets promoting a particular pro-life candidate on every windshield in the parking lot. When asked by the church leadership not to do this sort of thing again, the member was genuinely mystified. Her mystification grew from her failure to distinguish sufficiently between the responsibility of the individual Christian citizen and the responsibility of the institutional church.

Chapter two describes the primary calling of the church, a calling from which political matters must not divert it. But individual Christians, working alone and in conjunction with others, have more diverse callings. I must discern and pursue my particular calling, faithful to the One who intends to rule my whole life, both private and public. At the same time, I must not expect my church to adopt my calling and follow along after me, as if my priorities and those of my church ought to be precisely the same.

Distinguishing Between Principles and Strategies

This brings us to a third distinction—between principles and strategies. Shortly after a national election, one of the deacons in my church rose up in public worship and thanked God with these words: "O Lord, we bless you that at last your man is in the White House." His prayer drew a fiery response from another church member—a response that caused the deacon great surprise because of his failure to draw this third distinction. The institutional church (and the individual believer as well) must speak out on the standards and values that the King of the church loves. But the moment we move into the realm of strategy—the moment we begin to wrestle with just how we are to bring those standards and values to bear upon our culture—we must be careful, humble, and gracious with one another. My deacon was entitled to his conviction that Ronald Reagan was the best man for the White House at the time, but as a leader in the church, he needed to take care not to place divine sanction upon a fallen and imperfect instrument. God's law (the source of our highest principles) must not be compromised, but its application in public life (what we are calling strategies) must be left to the individual operating freely under the reign of Christ. One of the Scriptures' high principles is the sanctity of the human conscience in areas where biblical prescriptions are unclear or incomplete—and politics is invariably such an area.[7]

During the Nazi era, the church as the church had an obligation to resist Hitler in areas where he plainly broke God's law. The Confessing Church (to which Dietrich Bonhoeffer belonged) and portions of the Roman Catholic Church, especially in Bavaria, did just that. But Bonhoeffer's disturbing decision to participate in Hitler's assassination could never have been made by the institutional church, nor should that struggling patriot have asked the church to make such a decision.

In our day we wrestle with abortion. The institutional church has an obligation to resist abortion—to declare that human life from conception is from God and is to be defended. The Law of God says, "Thou shalt not kill," and so must the church.[8] But the institutional church has a further obligation to acknowledge that a host of different legitimate strategies (legislative and otherwise) exist for applying this principle. We might join the "rescue movement" (and go to jail), picket abortion clinics, offer sidewalk counseling to women as they approach a clinic, march for life, write political leaders, lobby for laws forbidding all abortions, lobby for laws forbidding abortion except in certain extreme circumstances, or vote for a certain candidate. We might approach the issue indirectly, laboring to develop feasible alternatives to abortion, or devote ourselves to dialogue with the opposition in hopes of finding a common ground that will at least reduce abortions.

Vive la Différence

Strategies vary tremendously, and believers should learn how to discuss those differences with each other in a spirit of love and humility. We should also bear with the church's reticence to endorse, or even to appear to endorse, one particular strategy, understanding that such endorsement fails to account for the diversity of gifts and callings that God gives his people and can divide the church where it should not be divided.

A good exercise, though it must never be entered into prayerlessly, is to hold churchwide public discussions on hot social issues, the purpose being twofold: to help one another distinguish between principles and strategies, and to learn how to debate and to disagree peaceably. The latter purpose is as important as the former, since we have been called to model the kingdom of God by our love. If we (in whom Christ dwells) cannot lovingly disagree, how can we expect the culture around us to?

A church in which I once served had a large medical population in its membership—medical students, medical school faculty and administrators, nurses, practicing physicians, and public health officials. Knowing that contemporary issues in medical ethics were on everyone's mind, we determined to have a class on the subject. We also knew that many of the issues involved were hot ones, potentially destructive to the fellowship of our church, so we proceeded cautiously. To prepare for it, a dozen of us (including me as the resident "theologian," the head of public health in the region, an administrator, some nurses, a researcher, and a number of practicing physicians) spent nearly a year together, studying and hammering out an understanding on a broad range of issues. The resulting class proved to be of immense help to scores of believers who were struggling with tough issues but were afraid to air them in church for fear of controversy.

Another church where I served would routinely hold Sunday evening panel discussions on hot topics. The wide range of issues included racism in the church, war, homosexuality, and women's leadership in the church and society. We generally chose the panelists from among ourselves so as to avoid a professional debate between outsiders. The aim was to learn how to speak honestly and charitably among ourselves.

William Wilberforce: A Model for Us

William Wilberforce grew up at a time when slavery flourished in the British Empire. Appalled by the practice, this young believer determined to fight it. Since he was a member of parliament and a gifted orator (providential realities that helped determine his public calling), Wilberforce settled upon a legislative strategy — to go after the institution by outlawing the trade. Humbled by his own complicity in the sin and by a keen sense of inadequacy, he opened the struggle in 1787 with this speech in the House of Commons:

> When I consider the magnitude of the subject which I am to bring before the House — a subject in which the interest, not of this country, nor of Europe alone, but of the whole world, and of posterity, are involved . . . it is impossible for me not to feel both terrified and concerned at my own inadequacy to such a task. But I march forward with a firmer step in the full assurance that my cause will bear me out. . . . I mean not to accuse anyone, but to take the shame upon myself, in common, indeed, with the whole Parliament of Great Britain, for having suffered this horrid trade to be carried on under their authority. We are all guilty — we ought all to plead guilty, and not to exculpate ourselves by throwing the blame on others.

Faced by an economy that depended heavily upon the continuation of slavery, he nevertheless clung tenaciously to the cause until after twenty years he saw the trade outlawed. For eighteen more years, until his retirement in 1825, Wilberforce fought unsuccessfully for the end of slavery itself. Not until July 29, 1833, three days before he died, did the bill abolishing slavery pass in the House of Commons. "Thank God," he whispered before he slipped into a final coma, "that I should have lived to witness a day in which England was willing to give twenty millions sterling for the abolition of slavery."[9]

Few of us may ever occupy the place of political influence that

Wilberforce held, and few of us may share his natural abilities. But we can all learn much from this remarkable statesman, a man whose faith was never disconnected from his public life. He challenges our pragmatism by being a man of undying principle who refused to allow staggering opposition and repeated failure to deter him. He challenges the impatient idealists among us by his patience and by his savvy willingness to go after slavery by going first after the slave trade (there is perhaps some wisdom here for the abortion struggle). He challenges those of us who have forgotten the legitimate role of religion in formulating public policy by being driven by Christian conviction throughout the struggle.[10] He challenges those among us who would withdraw from serious controversy, or simply lob mortars at the opposition, by readily accepting his nation's guilt as his own.

MAKING IT PERSONAL

1. Rousseau articulated a tension Christians often feel: "Jesus came in order to set up a spiritual kingdom on earth; thereby the theological system was separated from the political system, and this in turn meant that the state ceased to be *one* state, and that inherent tension emerged, which has never since ceased to agitate the Christian peoples." Discuss examples from your experience in which you have felt torn between allegiance to God and allegiance to your country. How did you resolve the tension?

2. In the fall of 1999 New York mayor Rudolph Giuliani sought to withhold city funds from the Brooklyn Museum when the museum chose to exhibit a painting of the Virgin Mary covered with cow dung. Some saw his action as a triumph for decency and godly values. Others saw it as an infringement on the freedom of expression. Still others complained that the mayor's action was foolish, playing into the publicity scheme of the exhibit's promoters. Was the mayor right to impose his views (and those of others) on the Brooklyn Museum?

3. Read the following excerpt from the chapter:

> We simply cannot escape the influence of values. They
> may be good values or bad values—depending upon our
> perspective—but they will always be the basis upon which we
> do our lawmaking. When, therefore, someone cries, "How dare
> you legislate morality!" what he or she really means is "How
> dare you legislate *that* particular morality, since I disagree with
> it." The proper question is not *whether* ethics should be
> enforced but rather *which* ethics should be enforced.

Discuss which social values should be enforced by law
and which should be promoted by other means. Try to
develop a rationale for the distinction.

4. According to this chapter, three distinctions will help us
think though the complex issue of legislating morality:

(a) the distinction between Christian influence and
Christian theocracy,

(b) the distinction between moral principle and political
strategy, and

(c) the distinction between the calling of the church as a
whole and the calling of the individual Christian.

Discuss what is meant by these three distinctions. Try to
develop a plan for addressing a hot social issue that takes all
of these distinctions into consideration.

5. Read over the final paragraph of the chapter, where the challenges of William Wilberforce are summarized. Evaluate your
own social and political involvements in light of Wilber-force's
example. Which are you more like: the pragmatist (who tends to
give up because the odds are long), the impatient idealist (who
demands perfection immediately), the secularist (one who has
"forgotten the legitimate role of religion in . . . public policy"), or
the "withdrawer" (who "simply lobs mortars at the opposition"
and refuses to accept "his nation's guilt as his own")?

LUKE 1:46-55

My soul glorifies the Lord
and my spirit rejoices in God my Savior,
for he has been mindful
of the humble state of his servant.
From now on all generations will call me blessed,
for the Mighty One has done great things for me—
holy is his name.
His mercy extends to those who fear him,
from generation to generation.
He has performed mighty deeds with his arm;
he has scattered those who are proud in their inmost
thoughts.
He has brought down rulers from their thrones
but has lifted up the humble.
He has filled the hungry with good things
but has sent the rich away empty.
He has helped his servant Israel,
remembering to be merciful
to Abraham and his descendants forever,
even as he said to our fathers.

Chapter Seven

MAKING A DIFFERENCE: THREE PRINCIPLES

I HAD NEVER THOUGHT MUCH ABOUT ABORTION UNTIL I HEARD C. Everett Koop, later to become the United States Surgeon General, address the issue in the late seventies. His lecture convinced my wife and me that our country was involved in an enormous social evil and we had to do something about it. But what? We hardly knew where to begin. It dawned on my wife, after some reflection, that she needed to part company with her gynecologist. This was not easy, since she was pregnant with our first child, and the gynecologist was a fine and attentive physician. But he actively promoted abortion rights and she could not in good conscience continue with him. Together we wrote him, communicating both our appreciation of his care and the reason for our departure from that care. He responded, as we expected he would (this is what made leaving him difficult), with a kind and gracious letter, explaining his position and wishing us well.

A number of years later, during the flap over the fatal decision a three-year-old's parents made to replace his conventional chemotherapy with something experimental, I wrote the following letter to the editor of *The Boston Globe*:

What is so striking is all the medical and legal uproar
over the life of one child when seen in the context of the
legally and medically sanctioned destruction of tens of
thousands of unborn children in Boston area hospitals
and clinics since 1973. Imagine for a moment that a test
had predicted Chad's condition before he was born.
Current wisdom might well have urged his destruction
"in utero" to save the family years of heartache and
expense. Since he was three years out of the womb, however, everything is different. Now the parents are at best
incompetent and at worst wicked. If Chad's parents had
shown "consistently bad judgment, which endangered
the life of their child" (Judge Hennessey), what of the rest
of us who have deliberately destroyed, or silently permitted the destruction of, so many unborn children? If we
are truly concerned about preserving life, then let's do so
consistently.[1]

In the mid-eighties, as the abortion debate continued to swell,
I grew increasingly troubled by the pro-choice complaint, often
justified, that the pro-lifers showed little concern for the mothers.
One Sunday I preached on the subject and was delighted when,
following the service, four University of Virginia law students
approached me asking what they could do. I really had no idea
but agreed to meet with them and talk over lunch. To my amazement, they ended up spearheading a "pro-mother" initiative that
led to the establishment of the Charlottesville Crisis Pregnancy
Center, a sensitive, practical, and professional ministry to women
with troubling pregnancies.

Most personally rewarding of all of our involvement in the
pro-life cause has been our relationship with Anne. A college
undergraduate, pregnant out of wedlock by a man who had no
long-term interest in her, Anne was under enormous pressure
from family and friends to have an abortion when she came to us.

She elected to keep the baby, and we elected to take her in. A woman in our church offered to be her Lamaze partner, accompanying her to all the classes and attending at the birth. Anne went on to finish her undergraduate studies, marry, and have at least one other child. A picture of her and her first child permanently adorns our refrigerator door.

Many Avenues
This brief account of my wife's and my involvement in a particular cause underscores something of the variety of avenues open to us as we work for change. Few of us have either the gifts or the opportunities that William Wilberforce had. But this should not discourage us, for legislative action at a national level is only one of many ways to bring about change. We serve a great God who works his will at every conceivable level of life and who especially likes to humble our proud hearts by working the greatest changes through the most unlikely means.

Think about Mary the mother of Jesus. A young Jewish woman in an occupied and male-dominated society, Mary had no social influence at all. Yet God called her to bear the one who would one day bring the whole earth to bow before his majesty. Filled with wonder, she celebrated in song a God who scatters the proud, brings down rulers, and sends the rich away empty while caring for and even exalting those who, like Mary, have no social clout (see Luke 1:46-55).

Like Gideon's tiny band, we are a strange army. But under God's hand, we can influence America profoundly. Consider some of the ways we can make a difference. We can talk up change, seeking to persuade by reasoned argument. Or we can live out change, seeking to demonstrate its wisdom by example. We can protest what we deem an unjust law, or seek to change it by legislative process. We can create the appetite for change through the arts (Billie Holiday's "Strange Fruit," a haunting jazz number about black lynching, stirred our national conscience). Or we can go after social change indirectly but most radically by throwing ourselves into evangelism. And we can work for change at a variety of different social levels, beginning with the smallest community (alone on our knees) and ranging upward from a conversation over coffee to a national debate. We must not mistakenly assume that the only road open to us is the limited-access highway of power politics (a way that, despite appearances, affects the deep things of culture only slightly). In a day when so many complain about their lack of empowerment, the believer who faithfully does what he or she can do, at whatever level, need neither worry nor complain.

The Principle of Respect

As we work, a number of important principles should help. We will consider five—three in this chapter and two in the next. They are the principles of respect, cooperation, diversity, integrity, and simplicity.

First, the principle of respect. We must, in other words, keep public life human. Whatever we do as American citizens, we must always act upon our heavenly King's operating principle that people matter more than politics or power. God used Mary for his purposes, but he never treated her as a cog in his cosmic machine. He spoke kindly to her through Gabriel, commending her and explaining what he was about to do. He sent the prophet Simeon to foretell her anguish. As Jesus hung dying, God saw to her comfort and protection by appointing John to look after her. In the Lord's modus operandi, the cosmic and the intimate, the big picture and the tiniest vignette of human experience come together. People have always mattered and will always matter supremely to him, even as he works out his great purposes.

Jesus' and the Apostles' Examples

First Peter 2:13 literally reads, "Submit yourselves for the Lord's sake to every human creature." Commenting on this statement, Edmund Clowney points out that "Peter is not talking about sub-

mission to institutions, but submission to people."[2] Peter human-
izes public life in keeping with God's priority. In doing so he
articulates what Christ demonstrated. For Jesus, political figures
were not merely (or even primarily) functionaries to be used, tolerated, placated, or somehow gotten around. They were individuals, people made in God's image, who needed to know the
heavenly King.

You perhaps remember the story of Nicodemus in John 3.
Nicodemus was a Pharisee and a member of the Jewish ruling
council—a member, in other words, of that group of people who
were Jesus' religious and political enemies. Jesus criticized this
group with such skill and vehemence that they came to hate him
passionately and eventually killed him. Yet when Nicodemus
came to Jesus by night, the Lord received him with respect and
directness. Jesus treated him not as a member of a particular
group but as a person in his own right.

Paul followed his Master's example when he was examined
before King Agrippa (Acts 26). On trial for his life, he appeared
in chains. Despite the adversarial setting, Paul brought the
interview to an end with sincere and simple words: "I pray God
that not only you but all who are listening to me today may
become what I am, except for these chains" (verse 29). For Paul,
Agrippa was above all a person for whom the prisoner wanted the
very best.

Such an attitude differs dramatically from what characterized
much of the social and political dealings in the twentieth century.
M. Y. Latsis, a leader in Lenin's secret police, the Cheka, wrote:

> The Extraordinary Commission is neither an investigating
> commission nor a tribunal. It is an organ of struggle,
> acting on the home front of the civil war. It does not
> judge the enemy: it strikes him. . . . We are not carrying
> out war against individuals. We are exterminating the
> bourgeoisie as a class. We are not looking for evidence or

witnesses to reveal deeds or words against the Soviet
power. The first question we ask is—to what class does
he belong, what are his origins, upbringing, education,
and profession? These questions define the fate of the
accused. This is the essence of the Red Terror.[3]

Lenin's decree of 1918 called on agencies of the state to
"purge the Russian land of all kinds of harmful insects," and
included in the list were, according to Aleksandr Solzhenitsyn,
"people in the Cooper movements, homeowners, high-school
teachers, parish councils and choirs, priests, monks, and nuns,
Tolstoyan pacifists, and officials of trade unions," all soon to be
classified as "former people."[4]

Lenin's political philosophy led to at least 20 million deaths
in Russia and set the precedent for similarly brutal purges in such
places as Germany, China, and Cambodia. With relief and
thanksgiving, we distance ourselves from such thinking and
sometimes forget how easily we gravitate toward less extreme
forms of the same thing. McCarthy's anticommunist movement in
the 1950s, the civil rights movement and its opponents in the
1960s, the politically correct movement in the 1990s, and the pro-
life movement (one could almost pick at random) have all to a
greater or lesser extent tended to identify the "enemy" as a group
and either repudiated or demonized them. While there is nothing
wrong with trying to understand and critique a movement or a
government as a whole, we often forget the most important
thing—that movements and governments are made up of people
who are made in God's image.

We must struggle to keep public life human. Endowed with
eyes of faith, we look through the bureaucracy and the power
structures to the people behind them. We try to look beyond the
badge to the heart and to practice respect, not only because of the
office represented but also because of the humanity of the one
who wears the badge. We try to look beyond the platform to the

people who align themselves with that platform, refusing to pigeonhole or demean or in any way dehumanize.

The End Never Justifies the Means

Government exists in God's plan to serve people, not to create by force or manipulation a utopia that those in power have imagined (utopias are God's business). We must therefore resist the temptation to allow the political end to justify the political means, particularly if this hurts people. God has freed us by the gospel to serve people, not to abuse them. Peter wrote, "Live as free men, but do not use your freedom as a cover-up for evil; live as servants of God. Show proper respect to everyone: Love the brotherhood of believers, fear God, honor the king" (1 Peter 2:16-17). Commenting on these verses, Edmund Clowney says,

> Christ's Lordship . . . must transform the way Christians exercise authority in [every] sphere of life. Christians will understand that political authority, like church authority, is service under God. Its purpose is the good of those governed, not the glory of the governor or the profit of the governing class. This principle guides Christians who share in governing authority in democracies. Their goal must also be to serve, to seek the good of the whole people, with special concern for the poor and weak.[5]

Though I have never held public office, I was appointed for a number of years to a steering committee whose purpose was to develop goals and standards for education in our school district. Frustrated by the snail's pace at which we often worked and the educational jargon we had to cope with, I often thought of quitting early. God helped me to persist by reminding me that the administrators, teachers, and community leaders with whom I worked were not primarily functionaries. They were creatures made in God's image responsible for the education of children, also made in God's image. They needed the perspective, prayers, and civility that an ambassador of Christ could bring to their work. I find it difficult to measure the success of the steering committee in its appointed task, but I am hopeful that something of the kingdom of God rubbed off on the people I worked with and that that was a good thing for our community.

Most of us have some degree of authority. You may be a police officer or a magistrate or an officer in the military. You may serve on your local school board or on an advisory committee to a government agency or on the student council. You may be an elected official with broad responsibilities. You may simply be a voter, set at liberty by our form of government to speak your mind and vote your conscience. Whatever your level of authority, exercise it with respect for people. For people will outlast every office and every institution. C. S. Lewis rightly observed that "nations, cultures, arts, civilization—these are mortal, and their life is to ours as the life of a gnat." When we understand this about people, we will resist the impulse to draw the human element out of public life. Whether I am confronting a bureaucrat at the Motor Vehicle Bureau, writing a senator whose recent vote disturbs me, discussing an issue at a school board meeting, talking over a hot public issue with a neighbor, evaluating American foreign policy, or considering how to vote on a referendum on prison reform, I will forever remember that politics is people dealing with people, and that people are immortals— "immortal horrors or everlasting splendors."[6]

The Principle of Cooperation

Respect fosters cooperation. If we understand that people always matter the most, we will seek to work *with* people as much as possible. We will struggle to be team players, encouraging others, looking for common ground, giving others the benefit of the doubt.

Ours is a suspicious day, prone to a we/they mindset, a mentality that poisons cooperation in public life. Christ wants us to bring healing, not disease. He calls us to be engaged in drawing the venom from public discourse by the manner in which we exercise our public responsibility.

At first glance Christian theology might seem to speak against cooperation. Scripture tells us that we are at war—that sin, the world, and the Devil implacably oppose the interests of God's kingdom. On what basis, then, can we work together with a fallen world? Three important doctrines answer this question: common grace, total depravity, and human creation in the image of God. The first doctrine, called "common grace," maintains that God continues to bless the world with his truth, beauty, and goodness despite our widespread rejection of him. Next, the doctrine of total depravity teaches that sin affects everything we do and everyone we meet. Third, the doctrine of creation in the image of God reminds us that every person matters profoundly.

A conspiracy mentality denies all three doctrines. In the first place it closes the mind to the possibility that "they" just might, on occasion, have a worthy insight, whether or not "they" acknowledge God as its source. It denies, in other words, that our merciful God often makes it possible for people with very different motives and worldviews to agree at a practical level—something I discovered to my amazement when I worked with a diverse group of educators, parents, clergy, and school administrators to develop standards of conduct in our local school.

In the second place, the conspiracy mindset forgets that sin reaches everywhere, even to the "good guys." "We" are no more exempt from the influence of spiritual darkness than "they" are.

In the third place, the conspiracy mentality simplifies complex matters by pigeonholing people ("Well, blacks are like that, you know!" "He's just a raving liberal!" "The religious right is nothing but bone-headed, selfish reactionaries!" "Women would never stand for this!"). Such sociological cloning overlooks the rich diversity among people and their opinions. It denies, in other words, the notion that God has made us in his image, one person at a time.

Of course, a ferocious and constant war rages. Scripture reminds us of this repeatedly (see Ephesians 6:12 and Revelation 12, especially verse 17). But according to the Bible, this war is not essentially between the church and the state, nor between the Christian and the government, nor even between the opposing factions in the culture wars. Good and evil are at war, and both of these realities show up everywhere—in the church and government, in Republicans, Democrats, and independents, in gays and straights, in Christians and nonChristians.

A law professor in my church once gave me some thoughtful advice in the midst of a discussion on the abortion issue. He asked, "Have you ever considered calling up the local president of the abortion rights movement and having a 'nonpolitical' cup of coffee together? You could tell her that you are pro-life but that your aim is not to argue; you want instead to listen and understand. She might be amazed to discover that you really care about the mothers involved in difficult pregnancies. Perhaps something positive might develop." So accustomed to the we/they approach had I become that such a thought had never crossed my mind.

James Hunter describes a number of cooperative agreements between pro-lifers and pro-choicers. One of them, which exists between Reproductive Health Services of St. Louis and Missouri Citizens for Life, grew out of the RHS director's invitation to the chief pro-life attorney to look for common ground together:

> As reported in the *New York Times*, " . . . when a pregnant 10-year-old came to the abortion clinic, but decided to carry her pregnancy to term, Jean Cavender, the clinic's director of public affairs and a participant in the common-ground talks, called Ms. Wagner [of Missouri Citizens for Life] for help. She told Ms. Wagner that the girl needed to stay in bed because the pregnancy was medically complicated but that because her mother worked there was no one to care for her during the day. Ms. Wagner then raised

enough money in anti-abortion circles to pay for an attendant and found a woman willing to go into the girl's dangerous drug-infested neighborhood. The baby was later put up for adoption."[7]

Who knows what good might come out of a concerted effort to cooperate like this?

Learning from George Washington

George Washington effectively brought people together. The delegates who gathered in Philadelphia in the sweltering summer of 1787 for what became the Constitutional Convention had many and profound differences of opinion on the ordering of the new union. The miraculous consensus that emerged owed at least as much to informal tavern talk as to formal public debate. Washington, who was silent in the latter, played a key role in the former. A biographer noted, "At the convivial gatherings, Washington was endlessly present, dining at one place, having supper at another, chatting between the acts of plays. He sought always to bring diverse points of view into the open and then together. History will never be able to assess the extent of the contribution Washington made through such personal contacts, but it was surely great. . . . He had, to a superlative degree, the gift for finding beneath controversy common ground."[8]

Like our first president, we should seek to be masters of cooperation. Without compromising our principles, we should always be on the lookout for common cause. We should pursue that common cause humbly, knowing that both our wisdom and our goodness must grow. We should seek to persuade rather than coerce, knowing that the former engages people in a more socially healthy search for common ground than does the latter. The principle of cooperation guides, in other words, the *tone* of our political and social involvement, a critical dimension to public life that we unfortunately do not often think much about.

Washington's cooperative spirit thrived on his genuine humility, the preeminent grace that seems to have made him, in James Flexner's terms, "the indispensable man."[9] In many of the crucial debates of his day, notably those in 1787 and 1788 over the ratification of the Constitution, he chose to remain silent, lest his immense prestige interfere with the experiment in self-governance at its start: "Washington became passionately eager to have the Constitution ratified. . . . As Washington watched [the state delegations debating], he again and again strained as on a leash to interfere. However, he had resolved to take no part in the debate."[10] When he did speak, his humble statesmanship moved and united people remarkably.

If we truly believe ourselves to be sinners, we will be the first to admit that we may be wrong. We will listen carefully and accuse rarely. We will build community rather than tear it down. We are told that Washington delivered his inaugural address "with trembling voice and trembling hands" and with an aspect that was "grave almost to sadness," qualities that deeply affected contemporary orators like Fisher Ames: "It seemed to me an allegory in which virtue was personified, and addressing those whom she would make her votaries. Her power over the heart was never greater."[11]

We must not forget what Washington understood and demonstrated so well: political solutions are rarely easy or obvious in our fallen world. To find them we must learn to work together humbly in common cause. The conspiracy mentality calls for an altogether different spirit, a mean and distrustful one. Such a spirit profoundly undermines the capacity for communication, constructive disagreement, and workable compromise — civic graces without which common cause is impossible.

We call ourselves sinners saved by grace, which means that we claim to have been humbled by the undeserved love of God. If we mean what we say, the conspiracy mentality will be alien to us. Grateful for God's mercy and alert to our own weakness, we will be slow to accuse and swift to build.

The Principle of Diversity

None of us is the same as anyone else. Our gifts, callings, and opportunities all differ. No two of us have the same amount or type of public clout, and therefore our activism as citizens will be splendidly diverse. This variation exists not only between people but also within the life span of each person. Consider, for example, the vast difference between Jesus' public role at his first coming and that at his second. Though opportunities for public influence varied over his lifetime,[12] Jesus never succeeded with the powers that be. A "mere" Jew, he had no influence with the Romans. Untrained and subversive, his only influence on the religious establishment was to enrage them. But one day this will all change. A day is in the offing (in fact, has already begun) when he will appear as reigning King of kings. No longer constrained by his God-given role as the Suffering Servant, he will receive the worship of every voice, human and angelic. His public opportunities will, in short, providentially and dramatically alter.

In his latter role, as in his former, Jesus will act obediently and trustingly in accordance with the opportunities that are providentially his. Herein lies our lesson. Like our Lord, all of us need to discern our present and unique public calling, and pursue it faithfully. And as part of that pursuit, we must cut some slack to our fellow Christians, none of who (even if they serve on the same committee) will have the same role as ours.

Finding Your Public Calling

How do you discern your public calling? First, assume that you have one (we are all called to be salt and light). Second, ask yourself, *What issues or matters in public life get my attention? What do I care about?* Third, consider your circumstances by asking, *What opportunities has God set before me in the areas where I have some interest?* Fourth, do something. In other words, take up one of the opportunities you have just discerned. You can't steer a boat that isn't moving. God defines and modifies our calling as we act.

When I agreed to serve on the goal-writing committee in our school district, I did so because I sensed a call to participate. By this I do not mean that God spoke audibly to me (he did not). Nor do I mean that every circumstance in my life pointed in that direction (I was already busy in my church responsibilities and I had no expertise in educational philosophy). What I mean is that opportunity, need, and interest came together sufficiently to persuade me that I should say yes to the invitation. For one thing, I had always had an interest in young people. For another, I had been for some time working with area clergy and school officials to draft a document on religion in the public schools. I knew that God wanted me to be involved in some way in my local community, and this particular way seemed to make sense.

In *Kingdoms in Conflict,* Charles Colson introduces us to Jack Eckerd and Trevor Ferrell, one the wealthy founder of a drugstore chain, the other an eleven-year-old boy. In 1983 Jack Eckerd went after pornographic magazines, pulling them from the seventeen hundred drugstores bearing his name, despite the financial risk, and urging other executives to follow suit. Eventually Revco, People's, Rite Aid, Dart Drug, High's Dairy Stores, and 7-Eleven did the same, largely through the initiative of one man who took to heart the public responsibility that attended the power providentially given him. In December of the same year that Jack Eckerd began his fight, Trevor Ferrell persuaded his parents to drive him into inner-city Philadelphia so that he could bring a blanket to a homeless person. That first visit led to many more visits and to a change not only in the Ferrell household, but also in their church and their community as more and more people became involved in "Trevor's Campaign." When asked by the media to explain his involvement, Trevor answered simply, "It's Jesus inside of me that makes me want to do this."[13]

Two very different people — one a wealthy businessman with a high degree of public clout, the other a boy with hardly any. What unites them is the choice each made to use his gifts and opportunities to bring the reign of Christ to bear upon his particular world. Their example encourages us to do the same, wherever our sphere of influence happens to be.

MAKING IT PERSONAL

1. Read over the Song of Mary (also called the Magnificat), the text of which appears in Luke 1 at the head of this chapter. List the social changes that she celebrates in her song. What do her words tell us about the sorts of social changes that matter most to God? Why is this so? Try to imagine how Mary must have felt, given her social clout at the time, to be chosen for her particular task. What can you learn from Mary's attitude, action, and perspective as you face social and political problems that are too big for you to handle?

2. Pick a social issue that is important to you and develop a plan for addressing it using (in addition to other strategies) the various strategies listed in the following statement from pages 91-92:

    We can talk up change, seeking to persuade by reasoned argument. Or we can live out change, seeking to demonstrate its wisdom by example. We can protest what we deem an unjust law, or seek to change it by legislative process. Or we can go after social change indirectly but most radically by throwing ourselves into evangelism. And we can work for change at a variety of different social levels, beginning with the smallest community (alone on our knees) and ranging upward from a conversation over coffee to a national debate.

3. The first principle in a balanced approach to social and political action is the principle of respect. Discuss ways to humanize your interaction with public officials like police officers, department of motor vehicle workers, senators, state assemblymen, school board members, and so forth. If you happen to be a public official, discuss ways to make your

dealings with your constituency more human and more responsive, especially to the poor and the less powerful.

4. The second principle is that of cooperation. This chapter describes three doctrines that should enhance our spirit of cooperation: (a) common grace, (b) total depravity, and (c) creation in the image of God. What do these doctrines teach and why do they motivate us to be more cooperative?

5. Think of a group whose social agenda really upsets you. Try to devise a plan for approaching that group peaceably and for cooperating with that group in some common endeavor.

6. The third principle is that of simplicity—doing what's doable for you. Try to define your own public calling. As you do so, be sure to ask for input from friends (we are always blind to certain things about ourselves). The following advice from the chapter should prove helpful:

First, assume that you have a calling (we are all called to be salt and light). Second, ask yourself, *What issues or matters in public life get my attention? What do I care about?* Third, consider your circumstances by asking, *What opportunities has God set before me in the areas where I have some interest?* Fourth, do something. In other words, take up one of the opportunities you have just discerned.

JOB 31:7-10,13-14,16,19,21-22, 26-28,33-34,38-40

If my steps have turned from the path,
    if my heart has been led by my eyes,
    or if my hands have been defiled,
then may others eat what I have sown,
    and may my crops be uprooted.

If my heart has been enticed by a woman,
    or if I have lurked at my neighbor's door,
then may my wife grind another man's grain,
    and may other men sleep with her.

If I have denied justice to my menservants and
        maidservants
    when they had a grievance against me,
what will I do when God confronts me?

If I have denied the desires of the poor
    or let the eyes of the widow grow weary,
if I have seen anyone perishing for lack of clothing, . . .
if I have raised my hand against the fatherless,
    knowing that I had influence in court,
then let my arm fall from the shoulder,
    let it be broken off at the joint.

If I have regarded the sun in its radiance
    or the moon moving in splendor,
so that my heart was secretly enticed
    and my hand offered them a kiss of homage,
then these also would be sins to be judged,
    for I would have been unfaithful to God on high.

If I have concealed my sin as men do,
*   by hiding my guilt in my heart*
because I so feared the crowd
*   and so dreaded the contempt of the clans*
*   that I kept silent and would not go outside,*
if my land cries out against me
*   and all its furrows are wet with tears,*
if I have devoured its yield without payment
*   or broken the spirit of its tenants,*
then let briers come up instead of wheat
*   and weeds instead of barley.*

Chapter Eight

INTEGRITY AND SIMPLICITY

I N JUNE 1939, GERMAN DISSIDENT DIETRICH BONHOEFFER SAILED TO America to teach and wait out the war in his homeland. But before long he found that his conscience would not permit him to remain in safety. Upon leaving for home less than a month later, he wrote to Reinhold Niebuhr:

> I have made a mistake in coming to America. I must live through this difficult period of our national history with the Christian people of Germany. I will have no right to participate in the reconstruction of Christian life in Germany after the war if I do not share the trials of this time with my people.[1]

Arrested in 1943 for his role in the German resistance, Bonhoeffer was hanged on April 9, 1945, one week before the allies liberated his prison.

When Martin Luther King Jr. set out to bring an end to segregation and voting injustice in Alabama and Mississippi, he faced enormous opposition. Fellow clergy spoke out against him.

From time to time, even close friends and allies sought to dissuade him. His house was bombed and close friends were killed. In the end he lost his own life. But these odds did not deter him from either goal or method.

Both Bonhoeffer and King were men of integrity. This does not mean that they were flawless (none of us is). Rather, it means that they were servants of the heavenly King who understood that pleasing him was more important than being safe or successful. It also means they resisted today's commonplace tendency to separate private living from public living. The whole of their lives belonged to Christ, not just the "spiritual" aspects. It was, in fact, their refusal to keep their faith private that got them into trouble.

Bonhoeffer and King could have traced their spiritual descent from Job. That ancient figure, whose final cry of innocence appears in partial form at the head of this chapter, seems to have known nothing of the fashionable modern distinction between public and private behavior. In one breath he spoke of sexual purity, ecological responsibility, purity of worship, justice in the courtroom, honesty in the marketplace, care for the poor, and guileless speech. Pursuing social justice and having a good devotional life carried equal weight for him because his life as a whole belonged to the God of all things.

So must it be with us. When our devotional life dries up, we nevertheless press on—because we know that it is good and healthy to pursue the Lord in prayer and meditation. Similarly, when our efforts to make our country and communities better places encounter opposition, we nevertheless keep at it because we know that our Lord loves justice and human love as much as he values prayer.

The Principle of Integrity

We must choose to do what is right simply because it is right, and not because it is always easy, popular, successful, or even (in extreme cases) lawful. Jesus encourages us in this by his example.

Though his public ministry began strongly, it ended in disaster from a worldly perspective. The adoring crowds deserted him and eventually turned on him.

Jesus "failed" because he would not compromise. Those who sought to trap him with the question on taxation spoke truly when they said, "Teacher, we know you are a man of integrity. You aren't swayed by men, because you pay no attention to who they are" (Mark 12:14). Jesus repeatedly confronted his followers with disturbing truths about themselves. He told them to forsake all in following him. He made a shambles of the temple courts because the commercialism there infuriated his Father. He exposed the greed, hypocrisy, and emptiness of the religious leaders. When on trial for his life, he told the truth about himself, even though he knew it would enrage his accusers and confirm in them their resolve to kill him. Such words and deeds were unpopular, but this made no difference to Jesus, since truth demanded the saying and the doing of them.

The apostles followed in their Master's footsteps. Beaten and jailed for preaching Christ and threatened with death if they continued, Peter and the others answered the authorities, "We must obey God rather than men!" (Acts 5:29; see verses 27-33). No doubt Peter said this respectfully, for we know that he saw all authority as coming from God. Nevertheless, with simple boldness and for the sake of the truth, he refused to obey. In this instance, giving God his due meant denying what "Caesar" demanded.

Such integrity can cost us our lives, as it did King and Bonhoeffer. It can land us in jail, as happened to many who chose to involve themselves in Operation Rescue. It may lose us some friends as my wife experienced when she politely refused to pay a friend "off the books" for housecleaning. On rare occasions, integrity makes public heroes of us, as it did Trevor Ferrell, the boy mentioned in the last chapter who handed out blankets to the homeless. Most of the time, however, we find it impossible to measure its impact. Usually God is the only one who sees.

Civil Disobedience?

In the Long Island town where I once lived, two historic churches face each other across the village green—Caroline Church of Brookhaven (Episcopal) and Setauket Presbyterian Church. A little over two hundred years ago, the Presbyterians watched with horror as the occupying British troops turned their building into a stable for their horses while they worshiped across the green at Caroline. Such desecration occurred because Episcopalians tended to be Tories and Presbyterians tended to be rebels. Two historic lessons present themselves: Christians have chosen to take up arms against the authorities that govern them, and Christians have differing opinions on when they may take such action.

May the principle of integrity ever lead to civil disobedience? I believe so. The apostle Peter told us to respect "the king" and "governors" because they "are sent by [God] to punish those who do wrong and to commend those who do right" (1 Peter 2:13-14). Implied in this high moral calling are grounds not only for critique but also for disobedience. When a government flagrantly violates God's description of its calling—when a government exalts evil and punishes good—grounds for disobedience exist.

In the century we have just left we have witnessed apartheid and the Holocaust. We have seen Austria, Czechoslovakia, Afghanistan, Chile, and many other nations overrun or destabilized by foreign countries. We have heard of Christian children being forcibly removed from their homes and brought up in atheistic institutions. We have had our fill of regimes that rewarded people for publicly lying and for denouncing their family, friends, and neighbors. We have been troubled by stories of people who have been punished by their governments for seeking to help fellow citizens escape oppression.

By God's grace, most modern Americans have not had to live directly under such oppression. But what of believers in other countries, or believers at earlier times in our own history? What about blacks in our own time? Bonhoeffer joined the plot to kill Hitler. In 1856 John Brown killed four pro-slavery settlers in his efforts to keep slavery out of Kansas. Harriet Tubman repeatedly broke the law in helping runaway slaves escape to the north, and the only reason she never used the pistol she packed seems to be that no one ever caught her. Martin Luther King Jr. acted in defiance of numerous court orders. Some Christians trespass on the grounds of abortion clinics in their protest against abortion laws. Members of Setauket Presbyterian Church, many of whom no doubt loved the Bible, took up arms against King George.

Violent and Nonviolent Resistance

Civil disobedience can be violent or nonviolent. Martin Luther King Jr. practiced the latter with great effect. To those (mostly fellow blacks) who complained that his approach was too passive, King distinguished sharply between "nonresistance to evil" and "nonviolent resistance," advocating the latter and contending that it can in fact be very aggressive and deliberate.

On December 1, 1953, Rosa Parks, a black woman, refused to surrender her seat to a white man who boarded the bus she was riding on. By her act, she broke the law in Montgomery, Alabama. Her arrest prompted King and others to call for a boycott of the city bus system. So effective was the boycott that it nearly bankrupted the bus company. King and many others were arrested and charged with violating antiboycott law. Following his conviction on March 22, 1956, King wrote:

> Ordinarily, a person leaving a courtroom with a conviction behind him would wear a somber face. But I left with a smile. I knew that I was a convicted criminal, but I was proud of my crime. It was the crime of joining my people in a nonviolent protest against injustice. It was the crime of seeking to instill within my people a sense of dignity and self-respect. It was the crime of desiring for

my people the unalienable rights of life, liberty, and the pursuit of happiness. It was above all the crime of seeking to convince my people that noncooperation with evil is as much a moral duty as is cooperation with good.[2]

Throughout those months, even when his home was bombed, King acted and counseled his many followers to act without violence. His cause and his method captured the attention of the nation, and on November 13, nearly a year after Rosa Parks refused to leave her seat, the United States Supreme Court declared Montgomery's law unconstitutional.

Violent Resistance?

Nonviolent resistance appeals to many Christians. But what about violent resistance? May a Christian ever protest injustice with force? If so, under what circumstances? How, for example, do I distinguish between the violence of John Brown and the (intended) violence of Dietrich Bonhoeffer? What is the difference between bombing an abortion clinic in 1976 and firing at British soldiers in 1776?

The answers to these questions are difficult and beyond the scope of this book. What we can say is that violent resistance may under certain extreme circumstances be permissible. It is conceivable that I may need to use violence to resist a greater violence, as did some ethnic Albanians living in Kosovo in 1999 when their nation's police burned their homes and murdered their kinfolk.

Violent resistance may be justifiable, but we should choose it with great reluctance, knowing that even bad governments exist by God's mercy to restrain the human race's natural tendency toward anarchy. If we ever choose violence, we should have first exhausted every other option, because we know that violence nearly always begets violence. We should recall the blood baths following the French and Russian revolutions, acknowledging that the overthrow of evil regimes has often opened the way to much worse ones. And we should repudiate the arrogance of claiming that we are God's holy warriors bringing in the kingdom of God through our acts of violence. In this regard Bonhoeffer has little in common with the self-styled prophet John Brown.

Integrity must characterize our public life. Results, publicity, our own safety, and peace must never be our primary concern but must rather be left in the hands of the one who has called us to leave all and follow him.

The Principle of Simplicity

Where do we begin? So many things cry out for attention that we can easily become overwhelmed. We resist being daunted by committing ourselves to the principle of simplicity. We will start by doing what is obvious and simple, rather than what is cosmic and subtle. "How do you eat an elephant?" asks the sage. His answer: "One bite at a time."

In the parable of the good Samaritan, Jesus taught that our neighbor, the proper object of our care, is anyone in need whom God has placed providentially at our feet. Care for that wounded man may have been inconvenient (there were other important things to do), socially unacceptable (Samaritans and Jews hated each other), even dangerous (bandits were known to lure victims by feigning injury on the Jericho road). But it was obvious and doable. Simplicity counsels us, "Before you rush off to develop a program that will provide better care for wounded travelers, or that will increase security on the Jericho road, take care of this particular man."

Some good friends of mine have taken a series of pregnant teenagers into their home. They have, in other words, addressed the abortion issue with simplicity, one child and one mother at a time. This is not to say that they have avoided other involvements. The principle of simplicity advises us on where to *begin* addressing a matter of public concern.

Nor is it to suggest that the obvious and the doable will be the same on a given issue for different people. Jack Eckerd's first step in fighting pornography might differ dramatically from that of a Christian clerk in one of his stores or a father who often shops there.

Two Stories

Because a church in which I once served is in a fairly affluent section of Long Island, we did not have access to homeless people unless we went in search of them. For this reason it came as something of a surprise to us when Dennis, rather "ripe" from too much alcohol and too little soap, joined us one Sunday morning for worship. Only mildly distracting during the first part of worship, he began crying out incoherently during the sermon. Uncertain of how to respond, I was relieved when two men and a woman arose from their seats and quietly removed the troubled man. I later learned that they had acted with no clear idea of what to do once they had removed Dennis; they had simply had a willingness to help as the Lord gave wisdom.

What began with the simple decision to do the obvious thing evolved, for one of the men, into something greater. Tim made friends with Dennis. He found him a place to live and over the next year saw him through both a detox and a literacy program. In the process our church came to know a number of homeless people and became involved in a soup kitchen ministry. Perhaps even more will come of Tim's decision to do the obvious thing. Who knows? This story will never draw media attention—it simply is not big enough. But I am convinced that it draws God's attention, for this is the way he usually advances his kingdom in the life of a nation.

A bigger and better-known story features Barbara Vogel's fifth-grade students at Highland Community School in Aurora, Colorado. In February 1998 she read them a newspaper article about the thriving and brutal slavery industry in Sudan. The students learned that that country's Islamic government makes war upon its own people, sanctioning raids on the non-Islamic Dinka villages to the south. The victorious raiders routinely carry off women and children and sell them into slavery.

So moved were Barbara Vogel's students that they researched the problem on the Internet to see if they could do anything about it. They discovered Christian Solidarity International (CSI), a Swiss organization that buys Sudanese slaves their freedom for about $50. Armed with this information, they undertook a campaign aimed at freeing Sudanese slaves, one at a time. According to a magazine report, "They collected allowance money, organized lemonade-stand sales, and sold used toys to raise money. After publicity on national television shows, the fifth graders, along with Vogel's new fourth-grade class last fall, began receiving individual and corporate donations from around the country. With every $50 raised, the students added a new brown-paper cutout of a freed slave to the classroom wall."[3] In seventeen months Vogel's young people raised $50,000 and fired a nationwide movement that has enabled CSI to redeem thousands. The striking thing about this remarkable effort is that it began so simply. A handful of students discovered a need to which they could relate (many slaves are the same age as their liberators), and they took steps to do what they could.

Mother Teresa's wise and powerful words, "Do small things with great love," bedeck one of Barbara Vogel's classroom walls. They remind us that there is always something we can do to make this world a better place.

Postscript

My church once sent me to Bangladesh to visit a number of the missionaries we support. India's eastern neighbor is an extremely poor Islamic country living constantly on the edge of political and economic disaster. In its brief history the country has experienced a series of severe famines and has rarely seen a change in political leadership that was not bloody. The believers there comprise less than 1 percent of the population. Full of remarkable faith and vitality, they have next to no influence politically and socially.

Within a week of my return from Bangladesh, I attended a

New York Rangers ice hockey game at Madison Square Garden with our son. When we rose to sing the national anthem, I was moved as I had never been before, thanks to my Bangladesh experience. For many in the stands that night, that song seemed to mean little more than a signal that the game was about to start. For me it was a reminder of the privilege and responsibility I possess as an American believer. Because I am an American, I belong to a political tradition that guarantees my freedom to assemble, to worship, and to speak and act according to conscience. Because I am a Christian, I have awesome responsibilities and mighty resources in the wise exercise of that freedom.

It is said that a woman approached Benjamin Franklin following the long session that produced the Constitution of the United States and asked him, "Sir, what is it going to be? A monarchy or a republic?" Franklin responded, "Madam, it is going to be a republic, *if* we can keep it." Neither Franklin nor the other founders of our noble and remarkable experiment in freedom ever assumed its perpetuity. They were public-spirited people who understood that the preservation of our "inalienable rights" depended on the public-spiritedness of those who would come after them. Perhaps more than anyone, Christians have reason for the inalienable rights we celebrate, for we know that God has created every human being in his image. Perhaps more than anyone, we have the power in Christ to exercise the love and respect necessary to promote and defend those rights. But that reason and that power will do very little to maintain our country's fragile freedom if we take that freedom for granted.

MAKING IT PERSONAL

1. Read Job's far-ranging testimony to his innocence in Job 31, and list fully the different areas of life that he covers. Inventory your own life in light of Job's list. Are there any areas that need scrutiny?

2. During the second term of his presidency, Bill Clinton was threatened with impeachment over a much-publicized affair with a White House intern. Some Americans argued that if a man cannot govern his private life, he should not be entrusted with governing a nation. Others argued that a president's private affairs are not the public's business and that his ability to govern a nation must be determined on other grounds (they occasionally alluded to other effective rulers who are known to have had affairs). Still others complained that all the hoopla was narrow and obsessive, as if the only ethics we should care about are sexual ethics. Discuss the affair and the public response in light of the principle of integrity.

3. Like his hero Gandhi, Martin Luther King Jr. practiced nonviolent resistance. Discuss the following statement from pages 111-112, made by King immediately following his criminal conviction:

Ordinarily, a person leaving a courtroom with a conviction behind him would wear a somber face. But I left with a smile. I knew that I was a convicted criminal, but I was proud of my crime. It was the crime of joining my people in a nonviolent protest against injustice. It was the crime of seeking to instill within my people a sense of dignity and self-respect. It was the crime of desiring for my people the unalienable rights of life, liberty, and the pursuit of happiness. It was above all the crime of seeking to convince my people that noncooperation with evil is as much a moral duty as is cooperation with good.

Why were King and Gandhi successful? Share and discuss examples of nonviolent resistance you have witnessed or participated in. Are there any present-day injustices that you believe call for nonviolent resistance?

4. What circumstances, if any, would prompt you to resist United States authority violently? What nonviolent means of

resistance would you have exhausted first? What form would your violent resistance take? What greater violence and injustice might your violence provoke?

5. The principle of simplicity calls us to change our world by behaving as the good Samaritan behaved, by doing whatever is obvious and doable. Share examples of this sort of action that you have seen or participated in. Is there anything obvious and doable that you or a group you are a part of can undertake?

6. Spend some time in prayer. Thank God for the many social and political freedoms you presently enjoy. Ask God for the sort of love, strength, perseverance, and wisdom that will enable you to make your community and country a better place.

APPENDIX A

B ELOW YOU WILL FIND THE TEXT OF THE WILLIAMSBURG CHARTER. Begun in the fall of 1986, it was revised over the course of two years in close consultation with a remarkably broad spectrum of political, academic, religious, and business leaders.[1] The framers presented it to the nation in Williamsburg, Virginia, on June 25, 1988 (the occasion of the two-hundredth anniversary of Virginia's call for the Bill of Rights), at which time the first one hundred national prominent figures signed it publicly. The charter celebrates and reaffirms the meaning of religious freedom in our pluralistic day and has helped me immensely as I have wrestled with the issues addressed in this book.

THE WILLIAMSBURG CHARTER: A NATIONAL CELEBRATION AND REAFFIRMATION OF THE FIRST AMENDMENT RELIGIOUS LIBERTY CLAUSES

Keenly aware of the high national purpose of commemorating the bicentennial of the United States Constitution, we who sign this

Charter seek to celebrate the Constitution's greatness, and to call for a bold reaffirmation and reappraisal of its vision and guiding principles. In particular, we call for a fresh consideration of religious liberty in our time, and of the place of the First Amendment Religious Liberty clauses in our national life.

We gratefully acknowledge that the Constitution has been hailed as America's "chief export" and "the most wonderful work ever struck off at a given time by the brain and purpose of man." Today, two hundred years after its signing, the Constitution is not only the world's oldest, still-effective written constitution, but the admired pattern of ordered liberty for countless people in many lands.

In spite of its enduring and universal qualities, however, some provisions of the Constitution are now the subject of widespread controversy in the United States. One area of intense controversy concerns the First Amendment Religious Liberty clauses, whose mutually reinforcing provisions act as a double guarantee of religious liberty, one part barring the making of any law "respecting an establishment of religion" and the other barring any law "prohibiting the Free Exercise thereof."

The First Amendment Religious Liberty provisions epitomize the Constitution's visionary realism. They were, as James Madison said, the "true remedy" to the predicament of religious conflict they originally addressed, and they well express the responsibilities and limits of the state with respect to liberty and justice.

Our commemoration of the Constitution's bicentennial must therefore go beyond celebration to rededication. Unless this is done, an irreplaceable part of national life will be endangered, and a remarkable opportunity for the expansion of liberty will be lost.

For we judge that the present controversies over religion in public life pose both a danger and an opportunity. There is evident danger in the fact that certain forms of politically reassertive religion in parts of the world are, in principle, enemies of democratic freedom and a source of deep social antagonism. There is also evident opportunity in the growing philosophical and cultural awareness that all people live by commitments and ideals, that value-neutrality is impossible in the ordering of society, and that we are on the edge of a promising moment for a fresh assessment of pluralism and liberty. It is with an eye to both the promise and the peril that we publish this Charter and pledge ourselves to its principles.

We readily acknowledge our continuing differences. Signing this Charter implies no pretense that we believe the same things or that our differences over policy proposals, legal interpretations, and philosophical groundings do not ultimately matter. The truth is not even that what unites us is deeper than what divides us, for differences over belief are the deepest and least easily negotiated of all.

The Charter sets forth a renewed national compact, in the sense of a solemn mutual agreement between parties, on how we view the place of religion in American life and how we should contend with each other's deepest differences in the public sphere. It is a call to a vision of public life that will allow conflict to lead to consensus, religious commitment to reinforce political civility. In this way, diversity is not a point of weakness but a source of strength.

I. A Time for Reaffirmation

We believe, in the first place, that the nature of the Religious Liberty clauses must be understood before the problems surrounding them can be resolved. We therefore affirm both their cardinal assumptions and the reasons for their crucial national importance.

With regard to the assumptions of the First Amendment Religious Liberty clauses, we hold three to be chief:

1. The Inalienable Right
Nothing is more characteristic of humankind than the natural and inescapable drive toward meaning and belonging, toward making sense of life and finding community in the world. As

fundamental and precious as life itself, this "will to meaning" finds expression in ultimate beliefs, whether theistic or non-theistic, transcendent or naturalistic, and these beliefs are most our own when a matter of conviction rather than coercion. They are most our own when, in the words of George Mason, the principal author of the Virginia Declaration of Rights, they are "directed only by reason and conviction, not by force or violence."

As James Madison expressed it in his Memorial and Remonstrance, "The Religion then of every man must be left to the conviction and conscience of every man; and it is the right of every man to exercise it as these may dictate. This right is in its nature an unalienable right."

Two hundred years later, despite dramatic changes in life and a marked increase of naturalistic philosophies in some parts of the world and in certain sectors of our society, this right to religious liberty based upon freedom of conscience remains fundamental and inalienable. While particular beliefs may be true or false, better or worse, the right to reach, hold, exercise them freely, or change them, is basic and nonnegotiable.

Religious liberty finally depends on neither the favors of the state and its officials nor the vagaries of tyrants or majorities. Religious liberty in a democracy is a right that may not be submitted to vote and depends on the outcome of no election. A society is only as just and free as it is respectful of this right, especially toward the beliefs of its smallest minorities and least popular communities.

The right to freedom of conscience is premised not upon science, nor upon social utility, nor upon pride of species. Rather, it is premised upon the inviolable dignity of the human person. It is the foundation of, and is integrally related to, all other rights and freedoms secured by the Constitution. This basic civil liberty is clearly acknowledged in the Declaration of Independence and is ineradicable from the long tradition of rights and liberties from which the Revolution sprang.

2. The Ever Present Danger

No threat to freedom of conscience and religious liberty has historically been greater than the coercions of both Church and State. These two institutions—the one religious, the other political—have through the centuries succumbed to the temptation of coercion in their claims over minds and souls. When these institutions and their claims have been combined, it has too often resulted in terrible violations of human liberty and dignity. They are so combined when the sword and purse of the State are in the hands of the Church, or when the State usurps the mantle of the Church so as to coerce the conscience and compel belief. These and other such confusions of religion and state authority represent the misordering of religion and government which it is the purpose of the Religious Liberty provisions to prevent.

Authorities and orthodoxies have changed, kingdoms and empires have come and gone, yet as John Milton once warned, "new Presbyter is but old priest writ large." Similarly, the modern persecutor of religion is but ancient tyrant with more refined instruments of control. Moreover, many of the greatest crimes against conscience of this century have been committed, not by religious authorities, but by ideologues virulently opposed to traditional religion.

Yet whether ancient or modern, issuing from religion or ideology, the result is the same: religious and ideological orthodoxies, when politically established, lead only too naturally toward what Roger Williams calls a "spiritual rape" that coerces the conscience and produces "rivers of civil blood" that stain the record of human history.

Less dramatic but also lethal to freedom, and the chief menace to religious liberty today, is the expanding power of government control over personal behavior and the institutions of society, when the government acts not so much in deliberate hostility to, but in reckless disregard of, communal belief and personal conscience.

Thanks principally to the wisdom of the First Amendment, the American experience is different. But even in America where state-established orthodoxies are unlawful and the state is constitutionally limited, religious liberty can never be taken for granted. It is a rare achievement that requires constant protection.

3. The Most Nearly Perfect Solution

Knowing well that "nothing human can be perfect" (James Madison) and that the Constitution was not "a faultless work" (Gouverneur Morris), the Framers nevertheless saw the First Amendment as a "true remedy" and the most nearly perfect solution yet devised for properly ordering the relationship of religion and the state in a free society.

There have been occasions when the protections of the First Amendment have been overridden or imperfectly applied. Nonetheless, the First Amendment is a momentous decision for religious liberty, the most important political decision for religious liberty and public justice in the history of humankind. Limitation upon religious liberty is allowable only where the State has borne a heavy burden of proof that the limitation is justified—not by any ordinary public interest, but by a supreme public necessity— and that no less restrictive alternative to limitation exists.

The Religious Liberty clauses are a brilliant construct in which both No Establishment and Free Exercise serve the ends of religious liberty and freedom of conscience. No longer can sword, purse, and sacred mantle be equated. Now, the government is barred from using religion's mantle to become a confessional State, and from allowing religion to use the government's sword and purse to become a coercing Church. In this new order, the freedom of the government from religious control and the freedom of religion from government control are a double guarantee of the protection of rights. No faith is referred or prohibited; for where there is no state-definable orthodoxy, there can be no state-punishable heresy.

With regard to the reasons why the First Amendment Religious Liberty clauses are important for the nation today, we hold five to be preeminent:

1. **The First Amendment Religious Liberty provisions have both a logical and historical priority in the Bill of Rights.** They have logical priority because the security of all rights rests upon the recognition that they are neither given by the State, nor can they be taken away by the State. Such rights are inherent in the inviolability of the human person. History demonstrates that unless these rights are protected, our society's slow, painful progress toward freedom would not have been possible.

2. **The First Amendment Religious Liberty provisions lie close to the distinctiveness of the American experiment.** The uniqueness of the American way of disestablishment and its consequences have often been more obvious to foreign observers such as Alexis de Tocqueville and Lord James Bryce, who wrote that "Of all the differences between the Old world and the New, this is perhaps the most salient." In particular, the Religious Liberty clauses are vital to harnessing otherwise centrifugal forces such as personal liberty and social diversity, thus sustaining republican vitality while making possible a necessary measure of national concord.

3. **The First Amendment Religious Liberty provisions are the democratic world's most salient alternative to the totalitarian repression of human rights and provide a corrective to unbridled nationalism and religious warfare around the world.**

4. The First Amendment Religious Liberty provisions provide the United States' most distinctive answer to one of the world's most pressing questions in the

late-twentieth century. They address the problem: How do we live with each other's deepest differences? How do religious convictions and political freedom complement rather than threaten each other on a small planet in a pluralistic age? In a world in which bigotry, fanaticism, terrorism, and the state control of religion are all too common responses to these questions, sustaining the justice and liberty of the American arrangement is an urgent moral task.

5. **The First Amendment Religious Liberty provisions give American society a unique position in relation to both the First and Third worlds.** Highly modernized like the rest of the First World, yet not so secularized, this society—largely because of religious freedom—remains, like most of the Third World, deeply religious. This fact, which is critical for possibilities of better human understanding, has not been sufficiently appreciated in American self-understanding, or drawn upon in American diplomacy and communication throughout the world.

In sum, as much if not more than any other single provision in the entire Constitution, the Religious Liberty provisions hold the key to American distinctiveness and American destiny. Far from being settled by the interpretations of judges and historians, the last word on the First Amendment likely rests in a chapter yet to be written, documenting the unfolding drama of America. If religious liberty is neglected, all civil liberties will suffer. If it is guarded and sustained, the American experiment will be the more secure.

II. A Time for Reappraisal

Much of the current controversy about religion and politics neither reflects the highest wisdom of the First Amendment nor serves the best interests of the disputants or the nation. We therefore call for a critical reappraisal of the course and consequences of such controversy. Four widespread errors have exacerbated the controversy needlessly.

1. The Issue Is Not Only What We Debate, but How

The debate about religion in public life is too often misconstrued as a clash of ideologies alone, pitting "secularists" against the "sectarians" or vice versa. Though competing and even contrary worldviews are involved, the controversy is not solely ideological. It also flows from a breakdown in understanding of how personal and communal beliefs should be related to public life.

The American republic depends upon the answers to two questions: By what ultimate truths ought we to live? And how should these be related to public life? The first question is personal, but has a public dimension because of the connection between beliefs and public virtue. The American answer to the first question is that the government is excluded from giving an answer. The second question, however, is thoroughly public in character, and a public answer is appropriate and necessary to the well-being of this society.

This second question was central to the idea of the First Amendment. The Religious Liberty provisions are not "articles of faith" concerned with the substance of particular doctrines or of policy issues. They are "articles of peace" concerned with the constitutional constraints and the shared prior understanding within which the American people can engage their differences in a civil manner and thus provide for both religious liberty and stable public government.

Conflicts over the relationship between deeply held beliefs and public policy will remain a continuing feature of democratic life. They do not discredit the First Amendment, but confirm its wisdom and point to the need to distinguish the Religious Liberty clauses from the particular controversies they address. The clauses can never be divorced from the controversies they address, but should always be held distinct. In the public discussion, an open commitment to the constraints and standards of the clauses should precede and accompany debate over the controversies.

2. The Issue Is Not Sectarian, but National

The role of religion in American public life is too often devalued or dismissed in public debate, as though the American people's historically vital religious traditions were at best a purely private matter and at worst essentially sectarian and divisive.

Such a position betrays a failure of civil respect for the convictions of others. It also underestimates the degree to which the Framers relied on the American people's religious convictions to be what de Tocqueville described as "the first of their political institutions." In America, this crucial public role has been played by diverse beliefs, not so much despite disestablishment as because of disestablishment.

The Founders knew well that the republic they established represented an audacious gamble against long historical odds. This form of government depends upon ultimate beliefs, for otherwise we have no right to the rights by which it thrives, yet rejects any official formulation of them. The republic will therefore always remain an "undecided experiment" that stands or falls by the dynamism of its nonestablished faiths.

3. The Issue Is Larger Than the Disputants

Recent controversies over religion and public life have too often become a form of warfare in which individuals, motives, and reputations have been impugned. The intensity of the debate is commensurate with the importance of the issues debated, but to those engaged in this warfare we present two arguments for reappraisal and restraint.

The lesser argument is one of expediency and is based on the ironic fact that each side has become the best argument for the other. One side's excesses have become the other side's arguments;

one side's extremists the other side's recruiters. The danger is that, as the ideological warfare becomes self-perpetuating, more serious issues and broader national interests will be forgotten and the bitterness deepened.

The more important argument is one of principle and is based on the fact that the several sides have pursued their objectives in ways which contradict their own best ideals. Too often, for example, religious believers have been uncharitable, liberals have been illiberal, conservatives have been insensitive to tradition, champions of tolerance have been intolerant, defenders of free speech have been censorious, and citizens of a republic based on democratic accommodations have succumbed to a habit of relentless confrontation.

4. The Issue Is Understandably Threatening

The First Amendment's meaning is too often debated in ways that ignore the genuine grievances or justifiable fears of opposing points of view. This happens when the logic of opposing arguments favors either an unwarranted intrusion of religion into public life or an unwarranted exclusion of religion from it. History plainly shows that with religious control over government, political freedom dies; with political control over religion, religious freedom dies.

The First Amendment has contributed to avoiding both these perils, but this happy experience is no cause for complacency. Though the United States has escaped the worst excesses experienced elsewhere in the world, the republic has shown two distinct tendencies of its own, one in the past and one today.

In earliest times, though lasting well into the twentieth century, there was a de facto semi-establishment of one religion in the United States: a generalized Protestantism given dominant status in national institutions, especially in the public schools. This development was largely approved by Protestants, but widely opposed by non-Protestants, including Catholics and Jews.

In more recent times, and partly in reaction, constitutional jurisprudence has tended, in the view of many, to move toward the de facto semi-establishment of a wholly secular understanding of the origin, nature, and destiny of humankind and of the American nation. During this period, the exclusion of teaching about the role of religion in society, based partly upon a misunderstanding of First Amendment decisions, has ironically resulted in giving a dominant status to such wholly secular understandings in many national institutions. Many secularists appear as unconcerned over the consequences of this development as were Protestants unconcerned about their de facto establishment earlier.

Such de facto establishments, though seldom extreme, usually benign and often unwitting, are the source of grievances and fears among the several parties in current controversies. Together with the encroachments of the expanding modern state, such de facto establishments, as much as any official establishment, are likely to remain a threat to freedom and justice for all.

Justifiable fears are raised by those who advocate theocracy or the coercive power of law to establish a "Christian American." While this advocacy is and should be legally protected, such proposals contradict freedom of conscience and the genius of the Religious Liberty provisions.

At the same time there are others who raise justifiable fears of an unwarranted exclusion of religion from public life. The assertion of moral judgments as though they were morally neutral, and interpretations of the "wall of separation" that would exclude religious expression and argument from public life, also contradict freedom of conscience and the genius of the provisions.

Civility obliges citizens in a pluralistic society to take great care in using words and casting issues. The communications media have a primary role, and thus a special responsibility, in shaping public opinion and debate. Words such as *public*, *secular,* and *religious* should be free from discriminatory bias. "Secular purpose," for example, should not mean "nonreligious purpose" but "general public purpose." Otherwise, the impression is gained that "public is equivalent to secular; religion is equivalent to private." Such equations are neither accurate nor just. Similarly, it is false to equate "public" and "governmental." In a society that sets store by the necessary limits on government, there are many spheres of life that are public but nongovernmental.

Two important conclusions follow from a reappraisal of the present controversies over religion in public life. First, the process of adjustment and readjustment to the constraints and standards of the Religious Liberty provisions is an ongoing requirement of American democracy. The Constitution is not a self-interpreting, self-executing document; and the prescriptions of the Religious Liberty provisions cannot by themselves resolve the myriad confusions and ambiguities surrounding the right ordering of the relationship between religion and government in a free society. The Framers clearly understood that the Religious Liberty provisions provide the legal construct for what must be an ongoing process of adjustment and mutual give-and-take in a democracy.

We are keenly aware that, especially over state-supported education, we as a people must continue to wrestle with the complex connections between religion and the transmission of moral values in a pluralistic society. Thus, we cannot have, and should not seek, a definitive, once for all solution to the questions that will continue to surround the Religious Liberty provisions.

Second, the need for such a readjustment today can best be addressed by remembering that the two clauses are essentially one provision for preserving religious liberty. Both parts, No Establishment and Free Exercise, are to be comprehensively understood as being in the service of religious liberty as a positive good. At the heart of the Establishment clause is the prohibition of state sponsorship of religion and at the heart of Free Exercise clause is the prohibition of state interference with religious liberty.

No sponsorship means that the State must leave to the free citizenry the public expression of ultimate beliefs, religious or otherwise, providing only that no expression is excluded from, and none governmentally favored, in the continuing democratic discourse.

No interference means the assurance of voluntary religious expression free from governmental intervention. This includes placing religious expression on an equal footing with all other forms of expression in genuinely public forums.

No sponsorship and no interference together mean fair opportunity. That is to say, all faiths are free to enter vigorously into public life and to exercise such influence as their followers and ideas engender. Such democratic exercise of influence as is in the best tradition of American voluntarism and is not an unwarranted "imposition" or "establishment."

III. A Time for Reconstitution

We believe, finally, that the time is ripe for a genuine expansion of democratic liberty, and that this goal may be attained through a new engagement of citizens in a debate that is reordered in accord with constitutional first principles and considerations of the common good. This amounts to no less than the reconstitution of a free republican people in our day. Careful consideration of three precepts would advance this possibility:

1. The Criteria Must Be Multiple

Reconstitution requires the recognition that the great dangers in interpreting the Constitution today are either to release interpretation from any demanding criteria or to narrow the criteria excessively. The first relaxes the necessary restraining force of the Constitution, while the second overlooks the insights that have arisen from the Constitution in two centuries of national experience.

Religious liberty is the only freedom in the First Amendment to be given two provisions. Together the clauses form a strong bulwark against suppression of religious liberty, yet they emerge from a series of dynamic tensions which cannot ultimately be relaxed. The Religious Liberty provisions grow out of an understanding not only of rights and a due recognition of faiths but of realism and a due recognition of factions. They themselves reflect both faith and skepticism. They raise questions of equality and liberty, majority rule and minority rights, individual convictions and communal tradition.

The Religious Liberty provisions must be understood both in terms of the Framers' intentions and history's sometimes surprising results. Interpreting and applying them today requires not only historical research but moral and political reflection.

The intention of the Framers is therefore a necessary but insufficient criterion for interpreting and applying the Constitution. But applied by itself, without any consideration of immutable principles of justice, the intention can easily be wielded as a weapon for governmental or sectarian causes, some quoting Jefferson and brandishing No Establishment and others citing Madison and brandishing Free Exercise. Rather, we must take the purpose and text of the Constitution seriously, sustain the principles behind the words and add an appreciation of the many-sided genius of the First Amendment and its complex development over time.

2. The Consensus Must Be Dynamic

Reconstitution requires a shared understanding of the relationship between the Constitution and the society it is to serve. The Framers understood that the Constitution is more than parchment and ink. The principles embodied in the document must be affirmed in practice by a free people since these principles reflect everything that constitutes the essential forms and substance of their society — the institutions, customs, and ideals as well as the laws. Civic vitality and the effectiveness of law can be undermined when they overlook this broader cultural context of the Constitution.

Notable in this connection is the striking absence today of any national consensus about religious liberty as a positive good. Yet religious liberty is indisputably what the Framers intended and what the First Amendment has preserved. Far from being a matter of exemption, exception, or even toleration, religious liberty is an unalienable right. Far from being a subcategory of free speech or a constitutional redundancy, religious liberty is distinct and foundational. Far from being simply an individual right, religious liberty is a positive social good. Far from denigrating religion as a social or political "problem," the separation of Church and State is both the saving of religion from the temptation of political power and an achievement inspired in large part by religion itself. Far from weakening religion, disestablishment has, as an historical fact, enabled it to flourish.

In light of the First Amendment, government should stand in relation to the churches, synagogues, and other communities of faith as the guarantor of freedom. In light of the First Amendment, the churches, synagogues, and other communities of faith stand in relation to the government as generators of faith, and therefore contribute to the spiritual and moral foundations of democracy. Thus, the government acts as a safeguard, but not the source, of freedom for faiths, whereas the churches and synagogues act as a source, but not the safeguard, of faiths for freedom.

The Religious Liberty provisions work for each other and for the federal idea as a whole. Neither established nor excluded, neither preferred nor proscribed, each faith (whether transcendent or naturalistic) is brought into a relationship with the government so that each is separated from the state in terms of its institutions, but democratically related to the state in terms of individuals and its ideas.

The result is neither a naked public square where all religion is excluded, nor a sacred public square with any religion established or semi-established. The result, rather, is a civil public square in which citizens of all religious faiths, or none, engage one another in the continuing democratic discourse.

3. The Compact Must Be Mutual

Reconstitution of a free republican people requires the recognition that religious liberty is a universal right joined to a universal duty to respect that right.

In turns and twists of history, victims of religious discrimination have often later become perpetrators. In the famous image of Roger Williams, those at the helm of the Ship of State forget they were once under the hatches. They have, he said, "One weight for themselves when they are under the hatches, and another for others when they come to the helm." They show themselves, said James Madison, "as ready to set up an establishment which is to take them in as they were to pull down that which shut them out." Thus, benignly or otherwise, Protestants have treated Catholics as they were once treated, and secularists have done likewise with both.

Such inconsistencies are the natural seedbed for the growth of a de facto establishment. Against such inconsistencies we affirm that a right for one is a right for another and a responsibility for all. A right for a Protestant is a right for an Orthodox is a right for a Catholic is a right for a Jew is a right for a Humanist is a right for a Mormon is a right for a Muslim is a right for a Buddhist—and for the followers of any other faith within the wide bounds of the republic.

That rights are universal and responsibilities mutual is both the premise and the promise of democratic pluralism. The First Amendment, in this sense, is the epitome of public justice and serves as the golden rule for civic life. Rights are best guarded and responsibilities best exercised when each person and group guards for all others the rights they wish guarded for themselves. Whereas the wearer of the English crown is officially the Defender of the Faith, all who uphold the American Constitution are defenders of the rights of all faiths.

From this axiom, that rights are universal and responsibilities mutual, derives guidelines for conducting public debates involving religion in a manner that is democratic and civil. These guidelines are not, and must not be, mandated by law. But they are, we believe, necessary to reconstitute and revitalize the American understanding of the role of religion in a free society.

First, those who claim the right to dissent should assume the responsibility to debate: Commitment to democratic pluralism assumes the coexistence within one political community of groups whose ultimate faith commitments may be incompatible, yet whose common commitment to social unity and diversity does justice to both the requirements of individual conscience and the wider community. A general consent to the obligations of citizenship is therefore inherent in the American experiment, both as a founding principle ("We the people") and as a matter of daily practice.

There must always be room for those who do not wish to participate in the public ordering of our common life, who desire to pursue their own religious witness separately as conscience dictates. But at the same time, for those who do wish to participate, it should be understood that those claiming the right to dissent should assume the responsibility to debate. As this responsibility is exercised, the characteristic American formula of individual liberty, complemented by respect for the opinions of others, permits differences to be asserted, yet a broad, active community of understanding to be sustained.

Second, those who claim the right to criticize should assume the responsibility to comprehend: One of the ironies of democratic life is that freedom of conscience is jeopardized by false tolerance as well as by outright intolerance. Genuine tolerance considers contrary views fairly and judges them on merit. Debased tolerance so refrains from making any judgment that it refuses to listen at all. Genuine tolerance honestly weighs honest differences and promotes both impartiality and pluralism. Debased tolerance results in indifference to the differences that vitalize a pluralistic democracy.

Central to the difference between genuine and debased tolerance is the recognition that peace and truth must be held in tension. Pluralism must not be confused with, and is in fact endangered by, philosophical and ethical indifference. Commitment to strong, clear philosophical and ethical ideas need not imply either intolerance or opposition to democratic pluralism. On the contrary, democratic pluralism requires an agreement to be locked in public argument over disagreements of consequence within the bonds of civility.

The right to argue for any public policy is a fundamental right for every citizen; respecting that right is a fundamental responsibility for all other citizens. When any view is expressed, all must uphold as constitutionally protected its advocate's right to express it. But others are free to challenge that view as politically pernicious, philosophically false, ethically evil, theologically idolatrous, or simply absurd, as the case may be seen to be.

Unless this tension between peace and truth is respected, civility cannot be sustained. In that event, tolerance degenerates into either apathetic relativism or a dogmatism as uncritical of itself as it is uncomprehending of others. The result is a general corruption of principled public debate.

Third, those who claim the right to influence should accept the responsibility not to inflame: Too often in recent disputes over religion and public affairs, some have insisted that any evidence of religious influence on public policy represents an establishment of religion and is therefore precluded as an improper "imposition." Such exclusion of religion from public life is historically unwarranted, philosophically inconsistent and profoundly undemocratic. The Framers' intention is indisputably ignored when public policy debates can appeal to the theses of Adam Smith and Karl Marx, or Charles Darwin and Sigmund Freud but not to the Western religious tradition in general and the Hebrew and Christian Scriptures in particular. Many of the most dynamic social movements in American history, including that of civil rights, were legitimately inspired and shaped by religious motivation.

Freedom of conscience and the right to influence public policy on the basis of religiously informed ideas are inseverably linked. In short, a key to democratic renewal is the fullest possible participation in the most open possible debate.

Religious liberty and democratic civility are also threatened, however, from another quarter. Overreacting to an improper veto on religion in public life, many have used religious language and images not for the legitimate influencing of policies but to inflame politics. Politics is indeed an extension of ethics and therefore engages religious principles; but some err by refusing to recognize that there is a distinction, though not a separation, between religion and politics. As a result, they bring to politics a misplaced absoluteness that idolizes politics, "Satanizes" their enemies, and politicizes their own faith.

Even the most morally informed policy positions involve prudential judgments as well as pure principle. Therefore, to make an absolute equation of principles and policies inflates politics and does violence to reason, civil life, and faith itself. Politics has recently been inflamed by a number of confusions: the confusion of personal religious affiliation with qualification or disqualification for public office; the confusion of claims to divine guidance with claims to divine endorsement; the confusion of government neutrality among faiths with government indifference or hostility to religion.

Fourth, those who claim the right to participate should accept the responsibility to persuade: Central to the American experience is the power of political persuasion. Growing partly from principle and partly from the pressures of democratic pluralism, commitment to persuasion is the corollary of the belief that the conscience is inviolable, coercion of conscience is evil, and the public interest is best served by consent hard won from vigorous debate. Those who believe themselves privy to the will of history brook no argument and need never tarry for consent. But to those who subscribe to the idea of government by the consent of the governed, compelled beliefs are a violation of the first principles. The natural logic of the Religious Liberty provisions is to foster a political culture of persuasion which admits the challenge of opinions from all sources.

Arguments for public policy should be more than private convictions shouted out loud. For persuasion to be principled, private convictions should be translated into publicly accessible claims. Such public claims should be made publicly accessible for two reasons: first, because they must engage those who do not share the same private convictions, and second, because they should be directed toward the common good.

RENEWAL OF THE FIRST PRINCIPLES

We who live in the third century of the American republic can learn well from the past as we look to the future. Our Founders were both idealists and realists. Their confidence in human abilities was tempered by their skepticism about human nature. Aware of what was new in their times, they also knew the need for renewal in times after theirs. "No free government, or the blessings of liberty," wrote George Mason in 1776, "can be preserved to any people, but by a firm adherence to justice, moderation, temperance, frugality, and virtue, and by frequent recurrence to fundamental principles."

True to the ideals and realism of that vision, we who sign this Charter, people of many and various beliefs, pledge ourselves to the enduring precepts of the First Amendment as the cornerstone of the American experiment in liberty under law.

We address ourselves to our fellow citizens, daring to hope that the strongest desire of the greatest number is for the common good. We are firmly persuaded that the principles asserted here require a fresh consideration, and that the renewal of religious liberty is crucial to sustain a free people that would remain free. We therefore commit ourselves to speak, write, and act according to this vision and these principles. We urge our fellow citizens to do the same.

To agree on such guiding principles and to achieve such a compact will not be easy. Whereas a law is a command directed to us, a compact is a promise that must proceed freely from us. To achieve it demands a measure of the vision, sacrifice, and perseverance shown by our Founders. Their task was to defy the past, seeing and securing religious liberty against the terrible precedents of history. Ours is to challenge the future, sustaining vigilance and broadening protections against every new menace, including that of our own complacency. Knowing the unquenchable desire for freedom, they lit a beacon. It is for us who know its blessings to keep it burning brightly.

Appendix B

B ELOW YOU WILL FIND THE TEXT OF A BROCHURE WE DEVELOPED and routinely distribute at the Three Village Church, a parish I served for twelve years. I offer it as an example of the sort of guidance churches should be giving to their people and as an inducement to produce better ones.

CHRISTIAN CITIZENSHIP: SOME PRINCIPLES AND PRACTICES

The Three Village Church

East Setauket, New York

Christians possess dual citizenship. They belong to the kingdom of God and they also belong to particular nations. In recent years much discussion (heated at times) has centered on how in practical terms we are to live out this dual citizenship. This pamphlet contains a series of 11 principles that the leadership of Three Village Church believes should govern our approach to these matters.

1. God is Creator and Lord of all things, and has called us to subdue all things to His glory. (Gen.1:1; Rev. 4:11; Gen. 1:28; Ro. 11:36; 1 Cor. 10:31)

Therefore, every sphere of life (including the political) is important and spiritual. Christians should seek to be informed of the political and social issues in our country and world.

2. God's Word is given to equip the Christian for every good work. (2 Tim. 3:16)

Therefore, there is no issue facing us that the Bible does not speak to in some way, and we must be careful not to single out any issue as uniquely worthy of the Christian's attention.

3. God has commissioned Christians to be "salt and light." (Mt. 5:13; Mk 9:50; Mt. 5:14; Mt. 5:16)

Therefore, every Christian should act upon his convictions in the social and political realms of life, employing all lawful means available. Furthermore, every Christian should be sensitive to how he or she acts; how we present our convictions is at least as important as the substance of our convictions.

4. The governments of this world are established by God as necessary evils to limit the potential reign of evil. (Ro. 13:1-7)

Therefore, the Christian citizen must work within the law, respecting it for God's sake, rather than because it is sound in every way. He or she must also respect all those who represent the law (police, magistrates, elected officials). There may be extreme instances warranting disobedience to the law, in which case the Christian should be willing to endure the consequences of law-breaking.

5. Jesus taught us to make a distinction between the kingdom of God and the kingdoms of this world,

reminding us that we have responsibilities to both. (The first, to which our deepest allegiance belongs, is international and spiritual, crossing all the barriers set by the second. It is enforced by the working of the Holy Spirit upon the heart through the Word of God.) (Mk. 12:17)

This distinction reminds us that we must resist the temptation to equate the United States or any human institution (past, present, or future—whether a nation or a political party or a government program) with God's kingdom.

This distinction implies further, that we limit our expectations regarding societal change through political means, remembering that the key to all such change is not a particular set of laws, or a party, or a government, but the working of the gospel in the hearts of people, one by one.

This distinction implies further that we see prayer as the primary and most powerful means of bringing change to society. We should pray, in particular, that rulers will maintain both social order and religious freedom of expression, since these are both necessary for the Word of God to be lived out and proclaimed. (1 Tim. 2:1-7)

6. The church of Jesus Christ, representing the present and coming reign of Jesus Christ, has been given a priority mandate to proclaim the gospel. (1 Pet. 2:9; Mt. 28:19-20)

Therefore, care must be taken that our involvement in political and social issues will neither divert us from this task nor divide us unnecessarily from each other or from those whom we are seeking to reach.

7. A distinction must be made in Christian thinking between the role of the individual Christian and the role of the "church-as-the-church" in addressing issues of Christian citizenship. The individual is free (and obligated)

to be involved in lobbying, voting, marching, etc. according to his conscience. The church-as-the-church, on the other hand, must preserve her primary task.

Therefore, our church will encourage people to be informed and active citizens, but will take care not to permit our corporate involvement in social and political issues to divert our attention unduly from fulfilling the Great Commission.

8. A distinction must be made in Christian thinking between principles and strategies. Principles are expression of moral law, and it is the duty of individuals and of the church-as-the-church to promote and uphold God's law. Strategies are the flawed and varied efforts we engage in to implement the moral law in society. In the realm of strategies the "church-as-the-church" must ordinarily give individual Christians the freedom and responsibility to discuss and act according to their own best judgment.

Therefore, the Three Village Church must be careful not to prescribe strategies, nor to give the impression that it is doing so.

9. Christians are ambassadors for Christ, exiles on earth, representing in public life their true King and homeland. (2 Cor. 5:20; 1 Pet. 2:11-17)

Christian citizens should therefore live exemplary public lives so as to give honor to their true Sovereign. They will never be content to limit their civic and social behavior by the questions, "Is it legal?" or "Can I get away with it?" They will always ask further questions, such as, "Is what I am doing moral?" and, "Does this please Christ?" and, "Will what I am about to do dishonor or inhibit Christ's place in the public mind?"

10. The Christian citizen is properly motivated by the desire to be faithful to God and not the need to see his

social/political agenda (however worthy) succeed.
(Ps. 46:10; 1 Sam. 24:1-3)

Therefore, he should patiently pursue what he deems right, even if the "right" never materializes. Furthermore, he should resist the tendency, born of impatience, to employ unworthy means to realize his dream more quickly.

11. The gospel champions the dignity of the individual and the freedom of the conscience. (Gen. 1:26-27; Ro. 14:23; 2 Cor. 5:11; 2 Cor. 9:7; 1 Tim. 2:1-2)

Therefore, the Christian citizen should continually ask, "How will my civic actions affect in the long run the freedom of all religious faith and practice in my country?" He will bear in mind that mixing politics and religion too tightly can violently polarize a nation and lead to the loss of religious freedom.

NOTES

Chapter One—First Principles

1. See Francis Fukuyama, "How to Re-Moralize America," *The Wilson Quarterly* 23, no. 3 (summer 1999), pp. 32-33.

2. See James Davison Hunter, *Before the Shooting Begins* (New York: Free Press, 1994), for an account of our present condition.

3. Václav Havel, "Forgetting We Are Not God," *First Things* 51 (March 1995), p. 48.

4. God distinguishes in Scripture between the premeditated killing of a person and accidental killing—a distinction that we find in our own law's distinction between murder and manslaughter. Abortion is, of course, premeditated, but for some people that act is not morally murder since they have been led to believe that what is aborted is not a person.

5. Quoted in Philip Yancey, *Church, Why Bother?* (Grand Rapids, Mich.: Zondervan, 1998), pp. 94-95.

6. The phrase "all the peoples" in verse 6 refers to all the different groups of people throughout the world.

7. People have different opinions on how Christian we were once, though it is fair to say that there was a time when a Protestant Christian ethos dominated the culture.

8. For this reason we must be wary of the sort of thinking that lifts an event or law out of ancient Israel's civic life and tries to insert it wholesale into the contemporary scene as "God's will for America." A particularly brutal and all too frequent example of this practice was to justify the conquest and killing of Indians as a modern-day version of the conquest of Canaan. In 1637, for example, Rev. Thomas Shepard described the bloody battles with the Pequots as "the divine slaughter of the Indians" at the hands of the Puritans.

9. Each of these quotes refers to actual situations, repeated in some cases many times. Happily the courts are beginning to reverse some of this trend. The "equal access" ruling, permitting student-run, voluntary Bible studies, is a case in point.

10. Ironically, the "wall of separation" language nowhere appears in the Constitution. Jefferson used it in an 1802 letter to a group of Baptists in Danbury, Connecticut, to

justify *federal* disengagement. "Recent research on Jefferson's letter (including the use of FBI computers to read beneath the ink he used to scratch out some of the original words) has shown that Jefferson was not so much hostile to government engagement with religion as he was to *federal* sponsorship of religion. Reasoning from Jefferson's scratched out words, Library of Congress archive director James Hutson has argued that this letter 'was never conceived by Jefferson to be a statement of fundamental principles.' Instead, it was a political document designed not to offend the strict separationists while leaving open tacit approval of *state* sponsored religious exercises. While Jefferson thought federal sponsorship of a day of prayer and thanksgiving was inappropriate, as a state governor, he himself called for such observances" (David Neff, "Can I Get a Witness," editorial in *Christianity Today*, August 9, 1999, pp. 26-27).

11. One need not be a religious relativist to acknowledge this. The Jesus who claimed he was the only way to the Father never forced anyone to believe him. He has no place in his kingdom for coerced disciples, but says instead, "I tell you the truth, whoever hears my word and believes him who sent me has eternal life" (John 5:24), and "Come to me, all you who are weary and burdened, and I will give you rest" (Matthew 11:28).

12. See Stephen L. Carter, *The Culture of Disbelief* (New York: Basic Books, 1993), for an excellent critique by a Yale law professor of our culture's tendency to trivialize the role of faith in public life.

Chapter Two—Keeping the Church Focused

1. Huge denominations, like the Roman Catholic Church, can perhaps take the risk more easily than independent community churches, since the former are known publicly to embrace a spectrum of opinions, whereas the only thing strangers will know about the latter will be what they see when they walk through the door.

2. E. J. Goodspeed, quoted by William Barclay in *The Gospel of Mark* (Philadelphia: Westminster, 1975), p. 287.

Chapter Three—Exemplary Ambassadors

1. Quoted in Christoph Schonborn, "The Hope of Heaven, the Hope of Earth," *First Things* (April 1995), p. 34.

2. James I. Packer, *A Quest for Godliness* (Wheaton, Ill.: Crossway, 1990), p. 14.

Chapter Four—Two Kingdoms

1. See Solomon's prayer at the dedication of the temple (1 Kings 8, especially verse 27). Note as well that non-Jews were routinely invited to join the commonwealth of Israel, thus reminding the Jews that, though he had chosen them, Yahweh had never ceased to be the Lord of all people (Numbers 15:13-16).

2. Antiochus Epiphanes was the pagan and murderous oppressor against whom Judas Maccabeus led his revolt.

3. The NEB captures the strong Greek verb well: "They heard him with astonishment."

4. Lord Acton, quoted by William Barclay in *The Gospel of Mark* (Philadelphia: Westminster, 1975), pp. 286-287.

5. Quoted in Tim Dowley, ed., *Eerdman's Handbook to the History of Christianity* (Grand Rapids, Mich.: Eerdmans, 1977), p. 363.

6. Augustine, *The City of God*, book XIV, chapter 4, trans. Henry Bettenson (New York: Penguin, 1972), p. 600.

7. John Howard Yoder, *The Politics of Jesus* (Grand Rapids, Mich.: Eerdmans, 1972), p. 190.

8. Yoder, p. 191.

9. Quoted in Dowley, p. 402.
10. The film features a platoon of soldiers commissioned shortly after the D-Day invasion to find Private Ryan (the last of four sons, all but him killed in battle) and to bring him safely home to his grief-stricken mother.
11. Augustine, who believed in the just use of violence, nevertheless grieved that any violence should be necessary: "The wise man . . . if he remembers that he is a human being . . . will rather lament the fact that he is faced with the necessity of waging just wars; for if they were not just, he would not have to engage in them, and consequently there would be no wars for a wise man. . . . Everyone who reflects with sorrow on such grievous evils, in all their horror and cruelty, must acknowledge the misery of them" (Augustine, pp. 861-862).

Chapter Five—Giving Caesar His Due

1. Antiochus IV (foreign ruler of Israel from 175 to 164 B.C.) took the name Epiphanes as shorthand for "god manifest." He sold the high priesthood to the highest bidder and, when the Jews rejected his choice, had Jerusalem sacked and its people slaughtered, after which he instituted frightful religious persecution: "Sabbath-keeping and the practice of circumcision were forbidden under pain of death, pagan sacrifices and prostitution were established in the temple, and law-loving Jews were subjected to every degradation and brutality" (A. F. Walls, *The New Bible Dictionary* [London: InterVarsity Fellowship, 1967], p. 762).
2. Ezra 1:2-4 contains Cyrus's decree.
3. Far from a pro-slavery manifesto, these words teach the nature of true freedom. Christian slaves only *appear* to be serving their earthly master; they in fact serve Christ and are therefore free from their human master's imperfections and injustices. Paul's words furthermore sow the seeds for emancipation, since the slaves' highest master is also the slave owners' master. The human masters who lived under Christ could not help but discover over time that they should not enslave another.
4. While in a Nazi prison, Bonhoeffer wrote a poem entitled "Who Am I?" A part of it reads, "Who am I? They often tell me/I used to speak to my warders/Freely and friendly and clearly/As though it were mine to command" (*Letters and Papers from Prison* [New York: Macmillan, 1962], p. 221).
5. Knowledge is power in our technology-dominated culture. Most things and events (even people) are seen as complex machines requiring experts to unlock their secrets. One such machine is modern legal practice.
6. Jean-Jacques Rousseau, *The Social Contract*, quoted by Schonborn, p. 32.
7. Charles Colson, *Kingdoms in Conflict* (Grand Rapids, Mich.: Morrow/Zondervan, 1987), p. 246.
8. Quoted in Iain H. Murray, *Jonathan Edwards* (Carlisle, Pa.: Banner of Truth Trust, 1987), p. 167.

Chapter Six—Giving God His Due

1. Tom Clancy, *The Sum of All Fears* (New York: Berkley, 1991), p. 18.
2. Genesis 1:26, "Let us make man in our image"; Romans 8:29, "For those God foreknew he also predestined to be conformed to the likeness of his Son."
3. Imagine that, immediately after his pronouncement about the Roman denarius, Jesus had asked for a baby to be brought to him and, holding it in his arms, had repeated the question "Whose image is *this*?" The proper, if shocking, answer (straight out of Genesis 1:26) would have been "It is God's image." And Jesus' rejoinder would have been "Then give this one fully to God."

4. Quoted in Schonborn, p. 32. The philosopher asserts that this divided loyalty leads to "a continuous struggle between the jurisdictions . . . which has made any reasonable civil order impossible in the Christian states." This observation may have had some historical validity at the time, though the success of the American "experiment," which Rousseau did not live to see (he died in 1778), provides a notable exception. We noted earlier that loyalty to Christ produces fine citizens.

5. Edmund Clowney, *The Message of 1 Peter* (Downers Grove, Ill.: InterVarsity Press, 1988), p. 109.

6. Ervin Duggan, "Pluralism That Makes a Difference," *First Things* (April 1995), p. 58.

7. See Romans 14 and 1 Corinthians 8 for lengthy discussions on the conscience.

8. Another biblical principle, of course, is mercy. The church that condemns abortion without also speaking and acting with love toward women who are ill-equipped to care for their children fails to bring all of the relevant biblical principles to bear upon the issue.

9. The source for my account of Wilberforce's battle against slavery is Colson, pp. 102, 105, 108.

10. The great evangelist John Wesley had written to Wilberforce, "Unless the Divine power has raised you up as *Athanasius contra mundum*, I see not how you can go through your glorious enterprise in opposing that execrable villainy, which is the scandal of religion, of England, and of human nature. . . . Oh, be not weary in well doing. Go on in the name of God, and in the power of His might." (Quoted in Colson, p. 105.)

Chapter Seven—Making a Difference: Three Principles

1. Charles Drew, letter to the editor, *The Boston Globe*, October 22, 1979, p. 9.

2. Edmund Clowney, *The Message of 1 Peter* (Downers Grove, Ill.: InterVarsity Press, 1988), p. 105. Clowney writes: "Many interpreters give another meaning to the word for 'creature.' They take it to mean 'order' or 'institution.' (The NIV expands this to 'authority instituted.') It is hard to find a clear example of this meaning outside the Bible, and it never means this in biblical usage. Peter is not talking about submission to institutions, but submission to people; to people, however, who have been given roles to fill in God's appointment. Our submission is to creatures of God made in his image."

3. Quoted in Paul Johnson, *Modern Times* (New York: Harper and Row, 1983), p. 70.

4. Quoted in Johnson, p. 70.

5. Clowney, p. 111.

6. C. S. Lewis, *The Weight of Glory* (Grand Rapids, Mich.: Eerdmans, 1972), p. 15.

7. Hunter, p. 232.

8. James Thomas Flexner, *Washington: The Indispensable Man* (New York: Little, Brown, 1969), p. 207.

9. Flexner, see title.

10. Flexner, p. 210.

11. Quoted in Flexner, pp. 217-218.

12. He grew up, increasing "in wisdom and stature, and in favor with God and men" (Luke 2:52), with all the normal fluctuations in influence that process implies. His brief sortie into the limelight at age twelve, his words amazing the scholars in the temple, ended abruptly when his parents recovered him. For eighteen years he lived in relative obscurity until God propelled him into a public ministry that ranged from widespread adulation to universal rejection.

13. Colson, p. 256. The accounts of Eckerd and Ferrell appear on pp. 262-263 and 255-257.

Chapter Eight—Integrity and Simplicity
1. Quoted in David P. Gushee, "Following Jesus to the Gallows," *Christianity Today*, April 3, 1995, p. 30.
2. Martin Luther King Jr., *Autobiography* (New York: Warner, 1998), pp. 87-88.
3. Christine Gardner, "Slave Redemption," *Christianity Today*, August 9, 1999, p. 28.

Appendix A—The Williamsburg Charter
1. Signers of the Williamsburg Charter include, but are not limited to, presidents Jimmy Carter and Gerald Ford, chief justices William Rehnquist and Warren Burger, senators Mark O. Hatfield and Daniel Patrick Moynihan, Nat Hentoff (columnist for *The Washington Post* and *The Village Voice*), Richard Neuhaus (director, Center for Religion and Society), Frank Fahrenkopf Jr. (chairman, Republican National Committee), Paul Kirk Jr. (chairman, Democratic National Committee), professors Peter Berger (Boston University) and William Van Alstyne (Duke University Law School), the Very Reverend Leonid Kishkovsky (president-elect, National Council of Churches), Rabbi Gilbert Klaperman (president, Synagogue Council of America), Archbishop John L. May (president, U.S. Catholic Conference), Imam Warith Deen Muhammad (Muslim American Community Assistance Fund), Adrian Rogers (president, Southern Baptist Convention), John H. White (president, National Association of Evangelicals), Elie Wiesel (Nobel laureate), Bishop Seigen H. Yamaoka (Buddhist Church of America), Donald Seibert (former chairman, J. C. Penney), Walter Cronkite, Coretta Scott King, Kyo Jhin (chairman, Asian-American Voter's Coalition), Derek Bok (president, Harvard University), Frank Rhodes (president, Cornell University), Albert Shanker (president, American Federation of Teachers), Wallace Jorgenson (chairman of the joint boards, National Association of Broadcasters), Horace Deets (executive director, American Association of Retired Persons), Frances Hesselbein (national executive director, Girl Scouts of the U.S.A.), Ben H. Love (chief scout executive, Boy Scouts of America), William Aramony (president, United Way of America), James Osborne (national commander, Salvation Army), Carmi Schwartz (executive vice president, Council of Jewish Federations).

ABOUT THE
AUTHOR

CHARLES DREW is a member of his local "Executive Committee of Education 2000" steering committee. He initiated a consortium of local clergy, school faculty, and administrators to bring about the adoption of "Religion in the Public Schools" which advocates religious pluralism in holiday celebrations and school curriculum. Drew is a Presbyterian minister who speaks regularly at universities, InterVarsity, and Campus Crusade events, FOCUS camps, and "The Fellowship," a large group of young Christian professionals in the Washington, D.C. area. He and his family live in Jersey City, New Jersey.